An Official V

UNITED STATES GOLD
COUNTERFEIT DETECTION GUIDE

BILL FIVAZ
Foreword by Randy Campbell

Whitman Publishing, LLC
Atlanta, Georgia

www.whitman**books**.com

© 2005 Whitman Publishing, LLC
3101 Clairmont Road · Suite C · Atlanta GA 30329

Correspondence concerning this book may be
directed to the publisher, at the address above.

ISBN: 0-7948-2007-7
Printed in Canada

For a complete catalog of numismatic reference books, supplies,
and storage products, visit Whitman Publishing online at
www.whitman**books**.com

About the cover: A tiny omega (Ω) is a counterfeit diagnostic—probably a counterfeiter's "signature"—found on some spurious $3 and $20 gold coins.

This book is dedicated to all the grading services. It is through their efforts and expertise that collectors can be assured that the vast majority of counterfeit gold pieces are detected and identified.

We all owe them a debt of gratitude for their dedication and their acumen in establishing the identity of these coins and keeping them off the market.

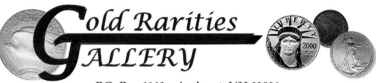

Bill Fivaz has been collecting coins since 1950, and today is one of the country's most respected authorities on numismatic errors and varieties. His numerous awards include the most prestigious recognition of the American Numismatic Association–the Farran Zerbe Award, presented in 1995. Bill is also a two-time recipient of the ANA Medal of Merit Award (1984, 1989). He was named a Krause Publications Numismatic Ambassador in 1982, and was recognized with the ANA Adult Advisor Award (for Young Numismatists) in 1991. He was also selected as the ANA Numismatist of the Year in 2001 and elected to the ANA Hall of Fame in 2002.

Bill has been an Educational Forum speaker at Florida United Numismatists conventions since 1979. As an instructor for the ANA's Summer Seminar for more than 25 years, he is considered by many to be a key to the program's great success. He has written hundreds of articles on a wide array of topics, and is a consultant to ANACS, SEGS, and several other authentication services. Bill's contributions are noted in many of today's most popular and respected hobby books, including the *Guide Book of United States Coins* (the "Red Book") and the *Comprehensive Catalog and Encyclopedia of Morgan and Peace Dollars* (by Van Allen and Mallis). He is co-author of *The Cherrypickers' Guide to Rare Die Varieties*, a classic now in its fourth edition.

Bill is a former member of the Board of Governors of the ANA, and a former member of the Board of Directors of CONECA (the Combined Organizations of Numismatic Error Collectors of America).

He has been married to his wife Marilyn for 50 years, and has a son (Bill), a daughter (Diane), two grandchildren (Erin and Jake), and a great-granddaughter (Ella).

B e afraid. Be *very* afraid! There are a great many counterfeit gold coins on the market, just waiting to be purchased by unsuspecting collectors and dealers.

How serious is the problem? I attended my first coin show in 1960. Since then, I have been at several hundred coin conventions of various sizes – and I have seen counterfeit gold coins *at every show I have attended*.

Since 1989, I have been a professional authenticator/grader for ANACS. I have spent roughly 3,500 days in the ANACS grading room, and on the vast majority of these days I have examined quantities of counterfeit and altered United States gold coins.

My best advice to all numismatists is this: *fight back*! Seek out the knowledge you need to combat the counterfeiters.

Much of the information you need may be found in Bill Fivaz's outstanding *United States Gold Counterfeit Detection Guide*. It is easy to read and easy to understand, and it is an absolute must for anyone who buys or is thinking of buying United States gold coins.

"Mr. Numismatic Education," Bill Fivaz, has done the hard work. This much-needed book is now a reality, so read, learn, enjoy, and share it with a friend.

Randy Campbell, NLG
ANACS Authenticator/Grader
Dublin, Ohio

You should be aware that many other counterfeit gold coins exist in the market than those covered in this book. The nearly 200 examples described here will educate you on what to look for, but be forewarned that no book will ever be able to illustrate *every* counterfeit.

When I first decided to write a book on counterfeit gold coins, I really didn't have a good confidence level on the subject, largely because I didn't collect gold and seldom looked at these coins at conventions, at coin shows, and at meetings.

I felt a reference book was badly needed, however, as there had not been one published on the subject in more than 30 years. As I researched, I sought the opinions of dealers and numismatists who collect, buy, sell, and trade in this segment of numismatics. Everyone agreed that this is a very serious problem, but because of the scope of the topic, no one had wanted to attempt a book-length study.

In researching the material for the *United States Gold Counterfeit Detection Guide*, out of necessity, I learned a great deal about what to look for, how to differentiate genuine specimens from counterfeits, and how to best present this new-found knowledge to the general numismatic community. The point is, I now have an infinitely better confidence level on gold, and I hope you will too, after reading this book.

The first counterfeit detection book I wrote years ago dealt with non-gold coins, and all the photos and diagnostics presented were of *genuine* specimens. In that reference book I felt it was better to teach readers the things to look for on genuine coins, and not confuse them with information on both legitimate and counterfeit pieces.

I decided that in this book, because there are so many different kinds of counterfeit coins that will fool collectors (and dealers), it would be more meaningful to illustrate and list the diagnostics of the pieces not to buy.

A surprisingly large number of the United States gold pieces currently on the market are counterfeit (as described by Randy Campbell in the foreword). Many of these counterfeit pieces have been produced overseas, and they usually contain gold of the proper weight and fineness. It is vital to be able to identify these coins and reject them when offered, so there won't be any unpleasant surprises when you or your heirs dispose of your collection.

This book shares several rules of thumb that should be kept in mind when examining a gold coin for authenticity. These are not hard-and-fast rules, but they will provide an excellent basis for your inspection. A glossary follows the Rules of Thumbs section. Next comes the meat of the book: a coin-by-coin study of examples within each circulating regular-issue denomination*, plus commemoratives and California fractional gold. The book concludes with an appendix of proper U.S. gold coin weights (an invaluable diagnostic), and an appendix showing features of genuine gold coins. Reading and studying all of these elements will give you a solid education in a potentially tricky but very rewarding field of the hobby.

Bill Fivaz
Dunwoody, Georgia

* $4 Stellas are not covered here as they are considered patterns, and not regular circulating issues. These coins, struck in 1879 and 1880, were rarely counterfeited. Any suspicious Stella should be submitted to one of the major independent grading services for authentication.

Acknowledgements

No book such as this can be published without the assistance and knowledge of a great many people. Reference coins for the illustrations were borrowed from many collectors and dealers. The expertise of these people, especially the authenticator/graders at ANACS, is greatly respected and appreciated. Michael Fahey made comments on many of the coins, and Randy Campbell and J.P. Martin (ICG) spent a great deal of time guiding me through the maze of deceptive counterfeits. Brad Rogers was also a tremendous resource, as he provided a great many coins for the book, complete with excellent diagnostics for each. My thanks to all these dedicated numismatists who offered their coins and expertise to help make this book a reality.

Several other people reviewed the manuscript and made excellent comments and suggestions. I am indebted to all these fine people for sharing their knowledge. This book is as much theirs as it is the author's.

CONTRIBUTORS

Al Adams
American Numismatic Association
Justin Atkins
Q. David Bowers
Kenneth Bressett
Bob Campbell
Randy Campbell (ANACS)
John Dannreuther
Tom DeLorey
Peggy Devine
Michael Fahey (ANACS)
Mike Faraone (PCGS)
Gary Fillers
Jeff Garrett
Steve Graham
Ron Guth
Don Hartlaub
David W. Lange (NGC)
Carl Lester
J.P. Martin (ICG)
Rick Montgomery (NGC)
Rob Moore
Don Paschal
David Patton
Brad Rogers
Mary Sauvain
Silvertowne
Anthony Swiatek
Fred Weinberg
Doug Winter

Rules of Thumb

Be sure to read this section, as it contains general guidelines relevant to the study of every counterfeit United States gold coin.

You should be aware that many other counterfeit gold coins exist in the market than those covered in this book. The nearly 200 examples described here will educate you on what to look for, but be forewarned that no book will ever be able to illustrate *every* counterfeit.

These are some rules of thumb to remember when examining gold coins for authenticity. These rules are not set in stone, but they provide excellent guidelines for your inspection. Note the close-up photographs in this section, and in the coin-by-coin section to follow.

Counterfeit Rules of Thumb

1. Weak/Fatty (W/F), mushy letters, devices. These are a good tip-off that the coin is not genuine. Legitimate specimens should have sharp, crisp numbers, letters, and devices. Many counterfeit gold pieces have this negative characteristic.

Weak/Fatty letters on a counterfeit quarter eagle.

Weak/Fatty letters on a counterfeit quarter eagle.

Weak/Fatty letters on a counterfeit gold dollar.

Weak/Fatty letters on a counterfeit commemorative gold dollar.

2. Repeating depressions. Primarily found in the fields of a coin, these should always be suspect, especially when they are of the same texture as the rest of the field and have soft, rounded edges. Repeating depressions are the result of legitimate contact marks on the genuine host coin (from which the false or one-to-one transfer dies were made). On the original specimen these were shiny depressions or abrasions with rather sharp edges, from where another coin or heavy object hit the coin. In order to effectively see these depressions, many of which are fairly subtle, it is imperative that after viewing the coin head-on, you twist, turn, and rotate it under a good incandescent light, often at a severe angle of 60° or more. This should enable you to pick up these and other negative features such as tool marks. *Note:* When "depressions" are used as a diagnostic in this text, it should be understood that they are repeating depressions, appearing on every counterfeit coin made by those dies.

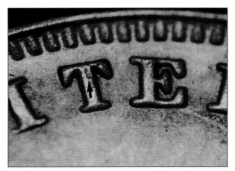

Depression on a counterfeit coin.

Depressions on a counterfeit coin.

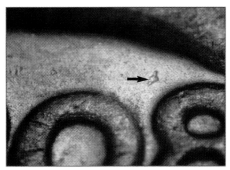

Depression on a counterfeit gold eagle.

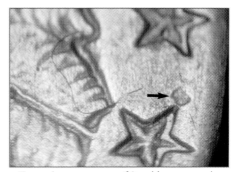

Depression on a counterfeit gold quarter eagle.

3

3. Tool marks. Worms are great for fishin', but not on gold coins! Many Indian Head $2½ and $5 gold counterfeits have worm-like, raised tooling marks (either straight or squiggly) at the back of the Indian's neck or above the necklace, as well as elsewhere on the coin. These marks are also found on other counterfeits of most denominations. They are the result of a counterfeiter's work on a false die. These two Indian Head series are generally considered among the most difficult to authenticate by collectors and dealers.

Tool marks on a counterfeit
Saint-Gaudens double eagle.

Tool marks on a counterfeit
Saint-Gaudens double eagle.

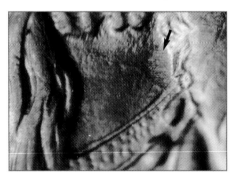

Tool marks commonly found on
counterfeit Indian Head quarter eagles
and half eagles (on the Indian's neck).

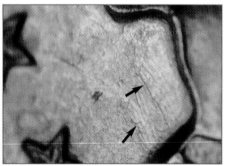

Tool marks on a counterfeit
Indian Head quarter eagle.

4. Spikes. In most cases, these tool marks running from the dentils on a coin are a good indication that it is not a genuine piece. However, this characteristic should not be used exclusively. Randy Campbell of ANACS states that in his estimation, about 3% of coins seen with spikes are actually genuine specimens. The (raised) spikes are usually seen leading from the dentil into the field and could be of various length and thickness. These are primarily found on the Liberty Head series (gold dollars through double eagles), especially on the later-date 19th- and early 20th-century coins. In some instances, spikes or tool marks may be found in the interior portions of the design.

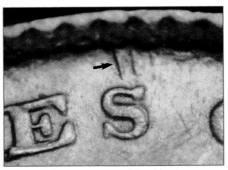
Spikes on a counterfeit gold coin.

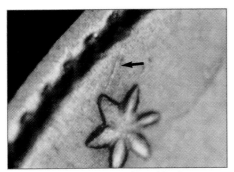
Spikes on a counterfeit gold coin.

Spikes on a counterfeit gold coin.

5

5. Sunken letters or numbers. These are not a good feature. If the centers of the letters or numbers appear to be depressed or concave (the "fallen cake syndrome"), chances are excellent that the coin is counterfeit. The 1811 Capped Bust $5 coin is a commonly seen counterfeit with these diagnostics. The counterfeit pictured here was analyzed by J.P. Martin and Bob Campbell at the 2005 ANA Summer Seminar. Their examination suggests that this and similar counterfeits were probably made from Great Britain sovereigns, as the gold content is identical (.917 fine).

Sunken numbers on a counterfeit
1811 Capped Bust half eagle.

6. Color. This is a very important factor in ascertaining the authenticity of a gold coin, but it is also probably the most difficult aspect to recognize by the average collector. Advanced collectors and dealers who specialize in gold can usually tell at arm's length if a coin is of the proper color for that date and mint. For example, branch mint gold coins struck in Charlotte, North Carolina usually have a reddish hue, while those minted in Dahlonega, Georgia or New Orleans, Louisiana often have a greenish color gold. Carl Lester, a specialist in Dahlonega gold, stated in his Spring/Summer 2003 *Georgia Numismatic Association Journal* article on the subject:

> Generally speaking, a gold coin with 100 parts per thousand copper alloy is distinctly orange in color. Gold coins with copper and silver tend to be less orange, and if the silver content is high enough, the coins do not look orange at all, possessing a light "green gold" color. As a consequence of this imprecise specification for the alloy, the mints at Dahlonega and Charlotte had the flexibility of having a higher silver content than the parent institution, the Philadelphia Mint.

Likewise, J.P. Martin (of ICG) advises that New Orleans and San Francisco counterfeits are mostly lighter in color because of the higher silver content, while those bearing the Philadelphia and (mostly) Denver mintmarks are generally more "coppery" due to the proper 90% gold/10% copper mix.

It is important to note that the color may also be affected by cleaning.

7. Variation of counterfeit characteristics. It may be the case that not all diagnostics illustrated for a given date will appear on all counterfeits for that date. Also, some counterfeits of the same date and mint in a series may have completely different diagnostics, depending upon the false dies from which they were struck.

8. Common, shared dies. Common non-dated reverse dies (and obverse dies on gold dollar and $3 pieces) were often used on different date counterfeits. The same holds true for false edge dies used on many Indian Head eagles and Saint-Gaudens double eagles.

9. Edge. Check the edge of gold coins for test marks, an indication that probably someone has questioned the coin's authenticity in the past. Also, Randy Campbell estimates that 3% to 5% of all pre-1834 gold coins were once jewelry pieces. Be sure to inspect them outside whatever holder they are in, so you can see if there is evidence on the edge of having been mounted in a bezel. Look also for discoloration on the rim and edge, from having been subjected to high heat. Also, be sure to examine the "third side of the coin" for irregular, uneven, or coarse reeding, which can be a giveaway for a counterfeit coin.

Rim and edge damage from jewelry mounting.

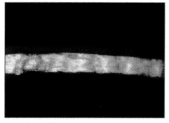

Edge of jewelry-mounted coin.

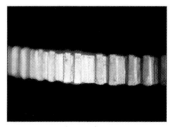

Irregular reeding on a counterfeit gold dollar.

"Fat," rounded reeding on a counterfeit gold dollar.

10. Weight. The weight of genuine coins should fall within the proper tolerances as indicated in Appendix A.

11. "Spinners." Some counterfeit Indian Head $5 pieces may "spin" when placed flat on a hard surface, due to one side being cup-shaped.

12. Mintmark. It is estimated that close to 90% of false Liberty Head gold coins are Philadelphia counterfeits (bearing no mintmark).

13. Greasy luster. Dave Bowers contributes the caveat that:

> …on many counterfeit coins the luster is sort of "greasy" and the fields of such issues as gold dollars and $3 pieces are often not properly prepared in the die-making process. Further, on genuine coins, the luster in the field is often of a different characteristic than the luster found on the portrait of Miss Liberty. On some counterfeits it is the same overall – again, rather "greasy" in appearance.

14. High-point luster and harsh cleaning. Jeff Garrett advises: "One of the most telling signs of a fake is a coin with wear that has complete 'luster' on the high points." Also, many times counterfeiters will harshly clean the coins to obscure the surface, making detection difficult.

15. Uncertified coins. Buying uncertified ("raw") coins on the Internet is like playing Russian Roulette with three bullets in the cylinder. Many sellers lack even basic counterfeit detection skills and could unwittingly sell you a counterfeit coin.

16. "Bubbles." A coin with bubbles on its surface is usually a cast counterfeit. The details are typically very weak and ill-defined and most often the color is incorrect.

Bubbles on a counterfeit gold quarter eagle. Bubbles on a counterfeit gold quarter eagle.

Genuine Coin Rules of Thumb

17. Genuine die wear. Characteristics associated with normal long die life (such as die erosion, wandering die cracks, and clashed die marks) are usually signs of a *genuine* coin. Refer to Appendix B for illustrations.

18. Microscopic detail. If you are really a serious collector of gold coins, it is highly recommended that you invest in a good-quality stereomicroscope so that you can see many of these diagnostics more clearly. It will pay for itself in a very short time.

19. Circulation wear. If the suspect coin is in Extremely Fine grade or lower, chances are in your favor that it is a genuine coin. This is not etched in stone, but it is a good rule of thumb.

20. Fine die polishing lines. Raised lines on the surface of a coin, in protected areas of its design (such as in LIBERTY on the headband), are usually a good sign that the coin is authentic. Refer to Appendix B for illustrations.

21. Certified coins. Before purchasing a coin, study some similar examples that have already been certified by the major grading services. The best opportunity to do this is at a coin show or at a dealer's shop. Pay particular attention to the color of the certified coins and the sharpness of their details. Also, Jeff Garrett notes that just because a coin is in a certified holder does not make it genuine. Some unscrupulous grading companies will holder counterfeit coins right alongside genuine ones. However, buying coins from reputable dealers, especially PNG (Professional Numismatists Guild) members, and coins that are encapsulated by the leading certification services' holders, offers a high degree of certainty of authenticity.

22. ANA courses. Take the American Numismatic Association's Counterfeit Detection Course, conducted at the annual Summer Seminar in June and July in Colorado Springs. You will have the opportunity for hands-on examination of both genuine and counterfeit gold coins, and benefit from the expertise of professional numismatists who know how to tell the differences.

23. Experienced opinions. Take full advantage of professional verbal opinions that are available at many of the larger coin conventions. ANACS has a table at most of these, and they are glad to help. Don't be hesitant to ask why they have reached their opinion. By doing this you'll expand your knowledge on the subject, which will make it easier to spot fakes in the future.

24. Overseas sellers. Never buy coins (especially gold) from overseas sellers you're not familiar with. Many fakes originate in foreign countries and retrieving a refund can be difficult or impossible.

25. Educational seminars. Presentations on counterfeit detection are also available at many coin conventions. Take full advantage of them!

26. Hobby periodicals. Some issues of *Numismatist*, *Coin World*, and *Numismatic News* have articles on counterfeit detection. Read them and cut them out – make your own "reference book" and review it often.

27. Study, study, study!!! Know what a genuine gold coin should look like by looking at as many slabbed specimens as you can. Note the crispness of their letters, numbers, and devices, their color and luster, and their surface qualities.

The following are terms used in this book and elsewhere in the study of counterfeit coins.

altered coin–A genuine coin that has had one or more elements of its design changed (e.g., a mintmark added or removed), usually to make it appear more valuable.

blemish (blem)–A raised lump of extra metal on a coin's surface.

bubble–A raised "pimple" on a counterfeit coin's surface, the result of having been produced by the casting method. Usually very crude and easily detected. Cast pimples differ from the smaller, raised pimples on a coin resulting from a rusted die.

cast coin–A coin cast in a mold that was made from a genuine coin. The main characteristics to look for are bubbles and "soft" letters and devices on the coin's surface.

counterfeit–A coin not produced by the United States Mint, resembling a regular-issue United States coin.

dentils (denticles)–The toothlike design element around the rims or borders of many coins.

die chip–A raised, unstruck area of planchet metal on a coin, caused by a small piece of the die breaking away.

hand-cut die–A die that has been hand cut by a counterfeiter to resemble a genuine Mint product. The coins struck by these dies will show subtle to very obvious design differences from those struck by a genuine die.

Kolit position (K-position)–A shorthand reference to the relative position on a coin of a certain feature, based on the numbers on the face of a clock. So named for Kolman and Litman, two numismatists who devised the identification term. Expressed as K-5 (5 o'clock), K-8 (8 o'clock), etc.

raw coin–A coin that has not been encapsulated in plastic by an independent grading service.

repeating depression–Usually found in a counterfeit coin's field, this is the product of normal contact marks on the genuine (host) coin from which the transfer dies were made. A repeating depression on a counterfeit is most often a shallow mark with rounded edges (a "soft dent") and a dull surface, similar to the surrounding field. Repeating depressions will appear on all coins struck from that die.

spike–An incuse file mark on a counterfeit die, normally toward the die's rim, left by its maker. Spikes show up as raised marks on the coin, usually as pointed "spears" emanating from the dentils into the field.

tool mark–A raised mark on a coin's surface, resulting from the counterfeiter's attempt to "clean up" blemishes on the counterfeit die. These are quite often found at the back of the neck on 1908 to 1929 Indian Head $2.50 and $5 coins.

transfer die–A die made by a counterfeiter from a genuine coin, then used to strike similar (but not legitimate) coins. Many of the negative characteristics of the genuine host coin, such as contact marks, will be transferred to the counterfeit die and will show up on all counterfeit coins struck from that die (see *repeating depression*, above). Transfer die counterfeits almost always show loss of detail.

W/F ("Weak/Fatty") letters and devices–Mushy, ill-defined, rounded letters, numbers, and other design elements; very common diagnostic of many counterfeit coins. The design elements of genuine coins usually have sharp, 90° corners, while those of W/F coins have rounded edges.

Gold Dollars

Be sure to read the Rules of Thumb on pages 1–9. They contain general guidelines relevant to the study of every counterfeit United States gold dollar.

You should be aware that many other counterfeit gold coins exist in the market than those covered in this book. The nearly 200 examples described here will educate you on what to look for, but be forewarned that no book will ever be able to illustrate *every* counterfeit.

1849 Open Wreath, Liberty Head $1

Obverse: Weak/Fatty stars and devices. Tool marks (spikes) from dentils at K-10 and K-4. Rough fields.

Obverse

Rough field; mushy stars, devices.

Spikes from dentils at K-10.

Spikes from dentils at K-4.

Reverse: Spikes above last S in STATES and over I in AMERICA.

Reverse

Spikes from dentils above S in STATES.

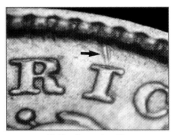

Spike from dentils over I in AMERICA.

1850 Liberty Head $1

Obverse: Small depressions on cheek and neck, and at star above Liberty's bun. Rough-surfaced fields.

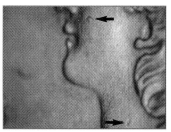

Depressions on cheek and neck.

Obverse

Depression at star above Liberty's bun.

Reverse: Raised lump near dentils above M in AMERICA. Slight depression in field next to lower right of 0 in date. Raised lumps in field to left of left ribbon end.

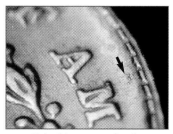

Raised lump near dentils above M in AMERICA.

Reverse

Depression next to 0 in date.

Raised lumps near left ribbon end.

1851 Liberty Head $1 (Example 1)

Obverse: Raised blems by stars at K-2 and K-6½.

Obverse

Raised blems by stars at K-2.

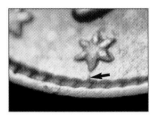

Raised blems by stars at K-6½.

Reverse: Depression over R and blem over O in DOLLAR. Depression above large 1 in denomination. Blem at K-5, between right bow ribbon and last A in AMERICA. Much of bow and ribbon design missing. Spike above D in UNITED. *Note:* The die crack through the D is not necessarily a counterfeit diagnostic for this coin, as genuine specimens sometimes exhibit this characteristic.

Reverse

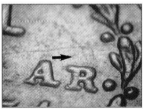

Depression over R in DOLLAR.

Depression over 1
in denomination.

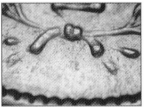

Missing elements
in bow and ribbon.

Blem over O in DOLLAR.

Blem near last A in AMERICA.

Spike above D in UNITED.

1851 Liberty Head $1 (Example 2)

Obverse: Blems by stars at K-11½ and K-2½.

Blem by star at K-11½.

Obverse

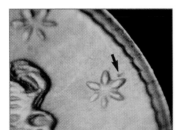

Blem by star at K-2½.

Reverse: Blem under 5 in date. Spike above E in STATES.

Blem under 5 in date.

Reverse

Spike above E in STATES.

1851 Liberty Head $1 (Example 3)

Obverse: Soft features (very mushy; not crisp) on Liberty and stars. Spikes from rim at K-8. Raised blems in hair at top of head.

Obverse

Soft features.

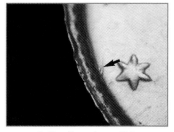

Spikes from rim at K-8.

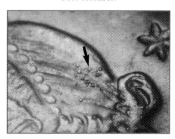

Blems in hair.

Reverse: Weak/Fatty letters and numbers. Spikes from rim throughout reverse, especially at K-9 and K-12. Raised blem under 5 in date.

Reverse

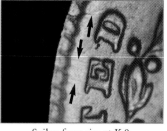

Spikes from rim at K-9.

Spike from rim at K-12.

Raised blem under 5 in date.

1852 Liberty Head $1

Obverse: Devices differ from those of a genuine coin. Wide and irregular rims. Pointed nose. *Note:* Made from a hand-cut die.

Detail of obverse.

Obverse

Pointed nose.

Reverse: Lettering, numbers, and devices differ from those of a genuine coin. Wide and irregular rims. Poorly formed leaves, date, etc. *Note:* Made from a hand-cut die.

Detail of reverse.

Reverse

Poorly formed date.

1852-O Liberty Head $1

Obverse: Repeating depressions in field behind Liberty's head, between stars. Spikes from dentils at K-4 and K-5.

Obverse

Depression behind head.

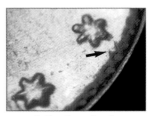

Spikes from dentils by star at K-4.

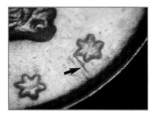

Raised line by star at K-4.

Reverse: Weak/Fatty letters and devices. Incomplete letters and mintmark.

Reverse

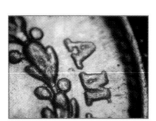

"Fat," mushy letters and devices.

"Fat" letters.

"Fat," mushy, incomplete letters.

Mushy letters; incomplete date and mintmark.

1853 Liberty Head $1 (Example 1)

Obverse: Depressions in field in front of face. Small, muted spikes around rim, especially at K-5½.

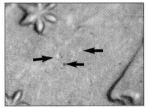

Depressions in front of face.

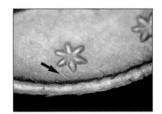

Small spikes around rim.

Obverse

Reverse: Depression to right of large 1 in denomination, near berry. Raised blem under N in UNITED. Raised blem to upper left of O in DOLLAR. Weak top of E in UNITED. Spike from dentils at K-6.

Depression to right
of 1 in denomination.

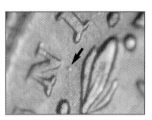

Raised blem under
N in UNITED.

Reverse

Raised blem to left
of O in DOLLAR.

Weak E in UNITED.

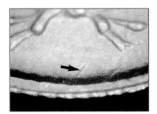

Spike from dentils at K-6.

1853 Liberty Head $1 (Example 2)

Obverse: *Note:* The severe raised lines by Liberty's ear and jaw are not counterfeit diagnostics for this coin; genuine specimens may exhibit this characteristic.

Obverse

Raised lines on face; not necessarily a counterfeit diagnostic.

Reverse: Raised lump below bow. Depression on large 1 in denomination. Blems (subtle raised lumps) in field above D in DOLLAR, near leaf.

Reverse

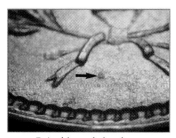

Raised lump below bow.

Depression on 1 in denomination.

Blems in field near leaf.

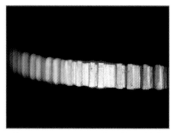

Edge: Be sure to examine the "third side" of the coin; this counterfeit has irregular reeding.

1853 Liberty Head $1 (Example 3)

Obverse: Depressions behind eye and at edge of hairline.

Depressions near eye and hairline.

Obverse

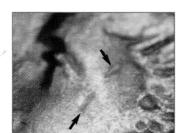

Closeup of depressions.

Reverse: Blem (lump) in field to upper left of 1 in date.

Blem near 1 in date.

Reverse

Closeup of blem.

1853 Liberty Head $1 (Example 4)

Obverse: Two short tool lines from dot between E and R in LIBERTY, and smaller ones after Y.

Obverse

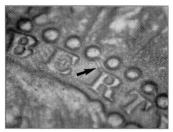

Tool lines between E and R in LIBERTY.

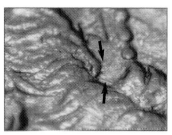

Small tool lines after Y in LIBERTY.

Reverse: Large depression to right of large 1 in denomination.

Reverse

Depression near 1 in denomination.

1853 Liberty Head $1 (Example 5)

Obverse: Devices different from those of a genuine coin. Sharp nose. Stars with "open" centers. Large die break on bust. *Note:* Made from a hand-cut die (different from the hand-cut 1852 counterfeit).

Detail of obverse.

Obverse

Open-centered stars.

Reverse: Lettering, numbers, and devices different from those of a genuine coin. Poorly formed letters and numerals in date. *Note:* Made from a hand-cut die (different from the hand-cut 1852 counterfeit).

Detail of reverse.

Reverse

Poorly formed letters and numerals.

1853 Liberty Head $1 (Example 6)

Obverse: Very wide rims. Long tool marks from star in front of face, and in front of forehead.

Obverse

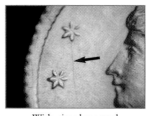

Wide rim; long tool mark in front of face.

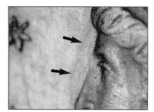

Tool marks in front of forehead.

Reverse: Depression above and between A and R in DOLLAR. Depression on large 1 in denomination. Tool mark above T in STATES. Tool mark at K-9, near UNITED.

Reverse

Depression above A and R in DOLLAR.

Depression on 1 in denomination.

Tool mark above T in STATES.

Tool mark at K-9.

1854 Liberty Head $1 (Example 1)

Obverse: Tool marks on lower bust.

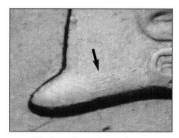

Tool marks on lower bust.

Obverse

Reverse: Tool marks above AME in AMERICA. Blem (raised lump) between U and N in UNITED.

Tool marks above
AME in AMERICA.

Reverse

Blem between U and N in UNITED.

Edge: Irregular reeding.

25

1854 Liberty Head $1 (Example 2)

Obverse: Tool marks in ear area; at K-4 (at rim); and at star at left, opposite Liberty's chin.

Obverse

Tool marks in ear area.

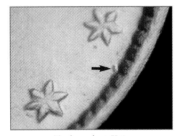

Tool mark at K-4.

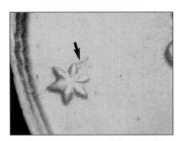

Tool mark at star near Liberty's chin.

Reverse: Tool marks around second T in STATES. Raised blem under same letter.

Reverse

Tool marks and blem around second T in STATES.

Edge: "Fat," rounded reeding.

1854 Liberty Head $1 (Example 3)

Obverse: Repeating depressions on cheek and throat.

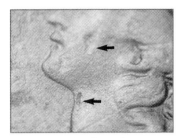

Repeating depressions
on cheek and throat.

Obverse

Reverse: Weak/Fatty, mushy letters. Tool marks near K-4, K-9, and K-12. Raised blems between R and I, between I and C, and above A, in AMERICA.

Tool mark at K-9.

Reverse

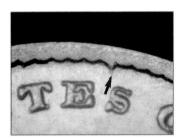

Tool mark at K-12.

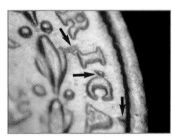

Raised blems around AMERICA.

1854 Indian Princess Head, Small Head $1 (Example 1)

Obverse: Line connecting A and M in AMERICA. Spike from dentils near last A in AMERICA.

Obverse

Line connecting A
and M in AMERICA.

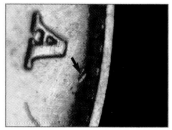

Spike from dentil
near final A in AMERICA.

Reverse: Tool marks (spikes) from dentils near wreath, at K-7.

Reverse

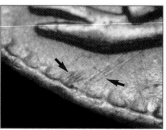

Spikes from dentils at K-7.

1854 Indian Princess Head, Small Head $1 (Example 2)

Obverse: Spike from dentil near R in AMERICA.

Spike from dentil
near R in AMERICA.

Obverse

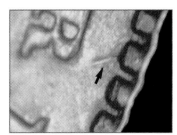

Closeup of spike.

Reverse: Depression between L and L in DOLLAR.

Depression between
L and L in DOLLAR.

Reverse

Closeup of depression.

1854 Indian Princess Head, Small Head $1 (Example 3)

Obverse: Tool mark near R in AMERICA. Blems around NIT in UNITED.

Obverse

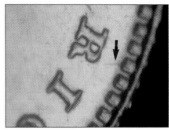

Tool mark near R in AMERICA.

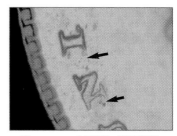

Blems around NIT in UNITED.

Reverse: Tool marks around lower wreath and at K-12.

Reverse

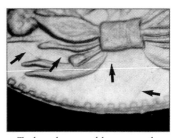

Tool marks around lower wreath.

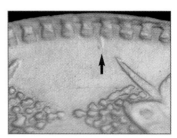

Tool mark at K-12.

1854 Indian Princess Head, Small Head $1 (Example 4)

Obverse: Weak/Fatty letters. Raised blems through UNITED.

Raised blems through UNITED.

Obverse

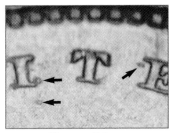

Closeup of blems.

Reverse: Tool marks (spikes) at K-6, K-7.

Spikes at K-6, K-7.

Reverse

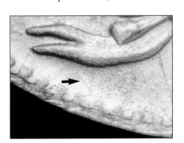

Spike at K-7.

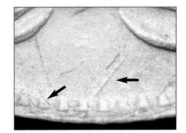

Spikes at K-6.

1855 Liberty Head $1

Note: This is a fantasy piece, produced from hand-made dies. Its composition is gold-plated base metal – not pure gold. No Liberty Head gold dollars were struck in 1855 (1854 was the final year of that design). There are several other known fantasy pieces that the reader should be aware of. Among these are: 1839 $5 in the Classic Head style (which actually ended in 1838); 1841-O $5 (with a spurious mintmark added); 1915-D Indian Head $5 (no authentic pieces were struck at Denver that year); 1904-S Liberty Head $10 (none were struck at San Francisco that year); 1909 Liberty Head $10 (the series actually ended in 1907); 1911 Saint-Gaudens "No Motto" $20 (the motto was introduced in 1908 and was included through 1932); and 1918 and 1919 Saint-Gaudens $20 (none were struck in those years).

Obverse

Reverse

1857 Indian Princess Head, Large Head $1

Obverse: Raised blem on jaw. Very subtle, large depression in field between STATES and OF. Tool marks through R in LIBERTY. Depression in field in front of nose.

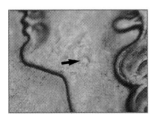

Raised blem on jaw.

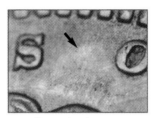

Depression between STATES and OF.

Obverse

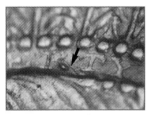

Tool marks through R in LIBERTY.

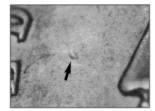

Depression in front of nose.

Reverse: Tool marks under right ribbon end.

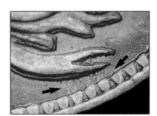

Tool marks through ribbon end.

Reverse

33

1862 Indian Princess Head, Large Head $1

Obverse: Spikes over first T in STATES. Raised blem in headband, where T in LIBERTY should be. Long, raised blem on jaw. Two small tool marks from lower right leg of R in AMERICA.

Obverse

Spikes over first T in STATES.

Raised blem in headband.

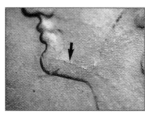

Long, raised blem on jaw.

Tool marks at R in AMERICA.

Reverse: Spikes from dentils at K-11. Ragged lumps below left ribbon, at K-7.

Reverse

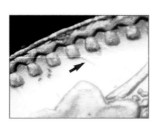

Spikes from dentils at K-11.

Lumps below ribbon at K-7.

1868 Indian Princess Head, Large Head $1 (Example 1)

Note: This is the most common date of counterfeit gold dollars.

Obverse: Weak/Fatty details (mushy letters, etc.). Long, raised die break from top of headdress to M in AMERICA.

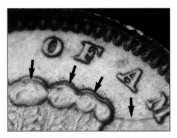

Die break near headdress.

Obverse

Reverse: Long die breaks through left and right sides of wreath.

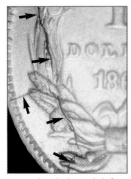

Die break through left
side of wreath and ribbon.

Reverse

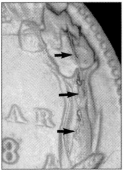

Die break through
right side of wreath.

35

1868 Indian Princess Head, Large Head $1 (Example 2)

Obverse: Weak/Fatty letters. Spikes all around obverse rim, especially over E in UNITED and over OF. Very weak I in AMERICA.

Obverse

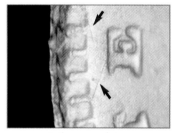

Spikes around rim.

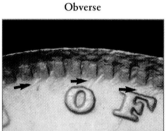

Spikes around rim.

W/F letters; spike around rim.

Reverse: Weak/Fatty letters in DOLLAR and numbers in date. Spikes all around reverse rim, especially under bow at K-6–7.

Reverse

Spikes around rim.

W/F letters and numbers.

1874 Indian Princess Head, Large Head $1 (Example 1)

Obverse: Depressed line from dentils between E and S in STATES to feathers. Many depressions in field behind head. Parallel raised arc lines in right field.

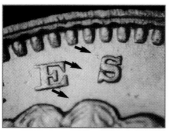

Depressed line between
E and S in STATES.

Obverse

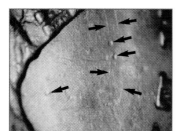

Depressions in field
behind head; raised arc lines.

Reverse: Depressions in field to left and right of large 1 in denomination. Spikes from rim at K-3.

Depressions near 1 in denomination.

Reverse

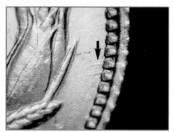

Spikes at K-3.

37

1874 Indian Princess Head, Large Head $1 (Example 2)

Obverse: Depression in field in front of neck. Raised tool line over U in UNITED, next to depressed groove over N. Depression between T and E in UNITED. Depression in field in front of forehead.

Obverse

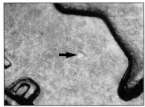

Depression in front of neck.

Tool line and groove next to U and N in UNITED.

Depression between T and E in UNITED.

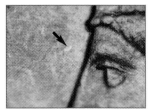

Depression near forehead.

Reverse: Depressed groove to upper left of large 1 in denomination. Depressed groove at top of 1 in date. Depression above DO in DOLLAR. Depression below left side of R.

Reverse

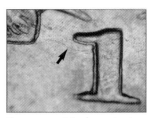

Groove near 1 in denomination.

Groove near 1 in date.

Depressions above DO and below R in DOLLAR.

1874 Indian Princess Head, Large Head $1 (Example 3)

Obverse: Blems (raised lumps of metal) above headdress, between and below last S of STATES and O of OF. Blems near dentil above and to left of O in OF. Depression between T and E in STATES.

Raised blems above headdress and in legend.

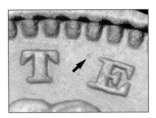

Depression between T and E in STATES.

Obverse

Reverse: Depression in lower part of large 1 in denomination. Filled (weak) O in DOLLAR. Small depression above wreath, near rim at K-12. Small depression in center of right wreath design, to right of R in DOLLAR.

Depression in 1 in denomination.

Filled (weak) O in DOLLAR.

Reverse

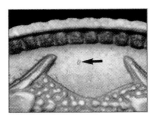

Depression above wreath.

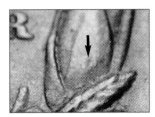

Depression in wreath.

1883 Indian Princess Head, Large Head $1

Obverse: Depression behind headdress, under first A in AMERICA.

Obverse

Depression behind headdress.

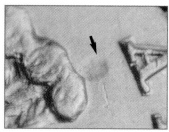

Closeup of depression.

Reverse: Depressions on large 1 in denomination.

Reverse

Depressions on 1 in denomination.

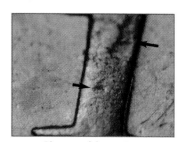

Closeup of depressions.

1887 Indian Princess Head, Large Head $1 (Example 1)

Obverse: Large, shallow depression at M in AMERICA. Tool marks (long, raised striations) from right dentils. *Note:* This is a common false obverse die used on many other counterfeit Indian Princess Head, Large Head gold pieces.

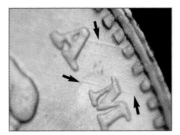

Depression at M in AMERICA;
tool marks from dentils.

Obverse

Reverse: Depressions in left field at K-9 and above large 1 in denomination.

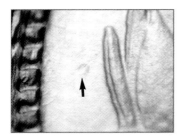

Depression at K-9.

Reverse

Depression above 1 in denomination.

1887 Indian Princess Head, Large Head $1 (Example 2)

Obverse: Weak/Fatty details. Small blem near dentil to left of O in OF. *Note:* This is a common false obverse die used on many other counterfeit Indian Princess Head, Large Head gold pieces.

Obverse

Blem near O in OF.

Reverse: Blem on lower left serif of R in DOLLAR. Depression in center of large 1 in denomination. *Note:* This is a common false reverse die used on many other counterfeit Indian Princess Head, Large Head gold pieces.

Reverse

Blem at R in DOLLAR.

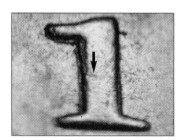

Depression on 1 in denomination.

1887 Indian Princess Head, Large Head $1 (Example 3)

Obverse: Fatty letters. Depression in field near R in AMERICA. Blem (raised lump) in field behind Liberty's headband.

Depression near R in AMERICA.

Obverse

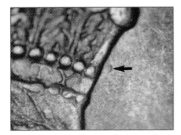

Blem near Liberty's headband.

Reverse: Depression in right field at K-3, near dentils. Depression on right side of bow knot. Blem on lower left serif of R in DOLLAR.

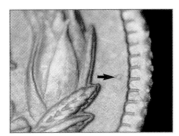

Depression at K-3.

Reverse

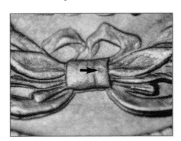

Depression on bow knot.

Blem at R in DOLLAR.

43

1887 Indian Princess Head, Large Head $1 (Example 4)

Obverse: Weak/Fatty letters and devices. Transfer of struck-through lint from original coin. Transfer of light die crack over head, also from original coin.

Obverse

Transfer of struck-through
lint from original coin.

Transfer of die crack
from original coin.

Reverse: Weak/Fatty letters and devices. Small depression over O on DOLLAR. Small depression under second 8 in date.

Reverse

Depression over O in DOLLAR.

Depression under date.

1888 Indian Princess Head, Large Head $1 (Example 1)

Obverse: No distinguishing diagnostics. Common obverse design, similar to regular-issue gold dollar.

Reverse: Depression on lower reverse below bow. Intermittent raised lines from K-4 to K-7.

Depression under bow;
raised line from K-4 to K-7.

Reverse

Closeup of depression
and raised line.

1888 Indian Princess Head, Large Head $1 (Example 2)

Obverse: Tool marks at back of neck and through AM in AMERICA. Depression at M in AMERICA. *Note:* This is a common false obverse die used on many other counterfeit Indian Princess Head, Large Head gold pieces (see also 1887, Example 1).

Obverse

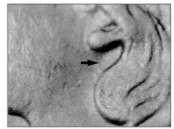

Tool mark at back of neck.

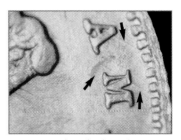

Tool marks through
AM in AMERICA.

Reverse: Long, raised tool mark (spike) from lower loop of last 8 in date up to leaf in wreath.

Reverse

Spike at date.

1888 Indian Princess Head, Large Head $1 (Example 3)

Obverse: Weak/Fatty details. Spike between T and E in STATES. Depressions to left of E and under R in LIBERTY.

Spike between T and E in STATES.

Obverse

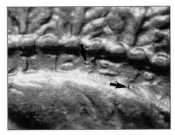

Depressions near letters of LIBERTY.

Reverse: Depression between A and R in DOLLAR. Several die cracks from dentils around reverse (K-6½, K-3, etc.).

Depression between
A and R in DOLLAR.

Reverse

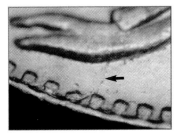

Die crack from dentil at K-6½.

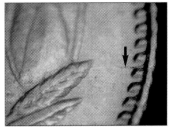

Die crack from dentil at K-3.

It's a new day at ANACS.

ANACS, America's oldest grading service, has undergone some exciting and new changes. We have redesigned our holder to be sleek, stylish, and Crystal Clear™. In addition, we have added new superstar graders to our grading team. In the coming months, be on the lookout for more exciting news from the company you know and trust. It's the dawn of a new day at ANACS.

- The sleek, state-of-the art holder is Crystal Clear™ and durable. It also offers you the unique ability to view the edge of the coin.

- ANACS graders have encyclopedic knowledge of coins backed by more than 125 years of combined grading experience.

- ANACS is The Collector's Choice® because we know what counts: knowledge, integrity, service, and trust. How much we value coin collecting is evident in our work.

Quarter Eagles

Be sure to read the Rules of Thumb on pages 1–9. They contain general guidelines relevant to the study of every counterfeit United States quarter eagle.

You should be aware that many other counterfeit gold coins exist in the market than those covered in this book. The nearly 200 examples described here will educate you on what to look for, but be forewarned that no book will ever be able to illustrate *every* counterfeit.

1850-D Liberty Head $2.50

Obverse and **Reverse:** Many raised blems all over coin. Very rough details. Slightly rotated dies. *Note:* This is a cast counterfeit; its weight is correct, but its "pimply" surfaces are a dead giveaway.

Obverse

Pimply surface and rough details.

Reverse

Pimply surface and rough details.

1861 Liberty Head $2.50

Obverse: Weak/Fatty features, especially on date. Blem in lower right field behind neck. Smaller blem between fourth and fifth stars on right.

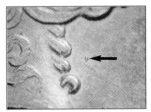

Blem behind neck.

Blem between stars at right.

Obverse

Reverse: Spikes from dentils at K-7 (under dot and near U and N in UNITED). Most letters doubled. Small raised blems between dentils and AMERICA. Long, depressed line through 2½. *Note:* This is a common false reverse die used on several other counterfeit Liberty Head quarter eagles (see also 1905, Example 2).

Spike from dentil at K-7; line through 2½.

Spike from dentil near U in UNITED.

Reverse

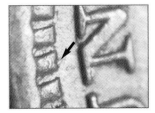

Spike from dentil near N in UNITED.

Raised blems between dentils and AMERICA.

Line through 2½.

1873 Liberty Head $2.50 (Example 1)

Obverse: Spike from dentils above star over top of hair bun at K-1. Small, round tool mark on center of cheek. Long die scratches (in an arc) through point of tiara on both sides. Fine, raised tool marks (scratches) in field over 8 in date.

Obverse

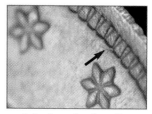

Spike from dentils at K-1.

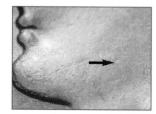

Tool mark on cheek.

Die scratches through tiara.

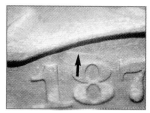

Tool marks near 8 in date.

Reverse: Thick spike from right base of first 2 in 2½ to dentil. More fine, raised tool lines through 2½ and in field above dot to left of that number. Heavy tool marks around AMER in AMERICA.

Reverse

Tool marks through 2½.

Tool marks around
AMER in AMERICA.

1873 Liberty Head $2.50 (Example 2)

Obverse: Weak/Fatty details. Depression near dentils at K-12. Several blems in and above upper hair area. Large blem over E in LIBERTY. Depression on lower bust. Tool marks under 1 in date.

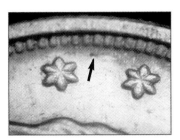

Depression at dentils near K-12.

Obverse

Blems in and above hair;
blem over E in LIBERTY.

Depression on lower bust;
tool marks under date.

Reverse: Weak/Fatty features; all letters, etc., very mushy. Depressions in field to lower left and right of eagle. Long, fine, straight lines in right field.

Depressions to left and right of eagle.

Reverse

Lines in right field.

53

1873 Liberty Head $2.50 (Example 3)

Obverse: Weak/Fatty (mushy) details throughout. Tool mark from dentils at K-7. Depressions on lower bust and jaw. Raised blem over head. *Note:* Made from a cast die.

Obverse

Tool mark from dentils at K-7; depression on lower bust.

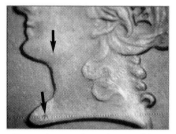

Depressions on lower bust and jaw.

Raised blem over head.

Reverse: Weak/Fatty features. Tool mark under 2½. *Note:* Made from a cast die.

Reverse

Tool mark under 2½.

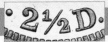

1879 Liberty Head $2.50

Obverse: Weak/Fatty diagnostics, especially in LIBERTY on tiara (fat letters). Very rough fields. Blem between fifth and sixth stars at left. Blem at point of bust. Depression on lower jaw.

W/F letters in LIBERTY.

Obverse

Blem between fifth
and sixth stars at left.

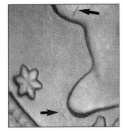

Blem at point of bust;
depression on lower jaw.

Reverse: Blem over eagle's left wing. Blem over D in denomination. Tool marks over TE in UNITED and through 2½.

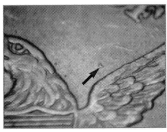

Blem over eagle's wing.

Reverse

Blem over D in denomination;
tool marks through 2½.

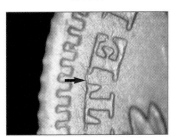

Tool marks over TE in UNITED.

55

1898 Liberty Head $2.50 (Example 1)

Obverse: Spikes from dentils by stars 1, 2, 3, 4, 7, 8, 9, 11, and 12.

Obverse

Spikes from dentils.

Spike from dentil.

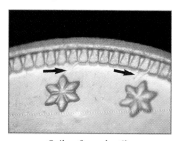

Spikes from dentils.

Reverse: Depression over eagle's head.

Reverse

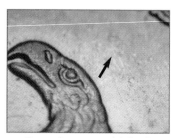

Depression over eagle's head.

1898 Liberty Head $2.50 (Example 2)

Obverse: Spikes by most stars. Depressions by fifth star on left; by sixth star on right; and behind bun.

Spikes near stars.

Obverse

Spikes near stars.

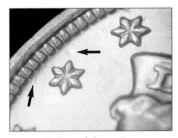

Spike and depression at fifth star on left.

Reverse: Depressions below 2½; in field behind eagle's head; and above arrow points. "Broken" bottom of D in denomination, after 2½.

Depressions below denomination; "broken" bottom of D.

Reverse

Depressions behind eagle's head.

Depressions above arrow points.

57

1902 Liberty Head $2.50

Obverse: Sharp nose. Different style of numerals in date. Irregular denticles. Irregular LIBERTY in tiara. *Note:* Made from a hand-cut die.

Obverse

Sharp nose; irregular lettering in LIBERTY.

Irregular date numerals and denticles.

Reverse: *Note:* Made from a hand-cut die.

Reverse

1903 Liberty Head $2.50

Obverse: Weak/Fatty features. Very shallow depression below first star on left.

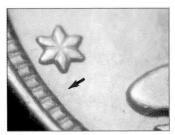

Shallow depression
below first star on left.

Obverse

Reverse: Weak/Fatty features (mushy letters, etc.).

W/F letters.

Reverse

Closeup of W/F letters.

1905 Liberty Head $2.50 (Example 1)

Obverse: Spikes from dentils at K-8.

Obverse

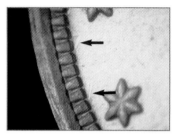

Spikes from dentils at K-8.

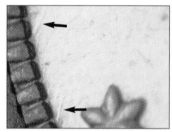

Closeup of spikes.

Reverse: Depression under eagle's right wing.

Reverse

Depressions under eagle's wing.

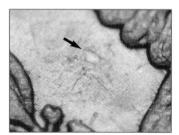

Closeup of depressions.

1905 Liberty Head $2.50 (Example 2)

Obverse: Depressions below 0 and over 5 in date. Depression in field behind neck.

Depressions at date.

Obverse

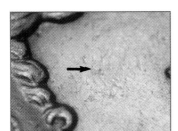

Depression behind neck.

Reverse: Depressed line through 2½. Spike from rim at K-7. *Note:* This is a common false reverse die used on several other counterfeit Liberty Head quarter eagles (see also 1861).

Line through 2½; spike at K-7.

Reverse

1906 Liberty Head $2.50 (Example 1)

Obverse: Depression on cheek. Shallow raised blems between 0 and 6 in date, and to lower right of 6.

Obverse

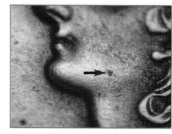

Depression on cheek.

Blems at date.

Reverse: Depression under O in OF. Depression in right field above arrow points.

Reverse

Depression under O in OF.

Depression above arrow points.

1906 Liberty Head $2.50 (Example 2)

Obverse: Spikes from dentils to left of date and over first six stars on right.

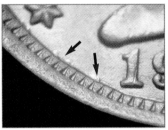

Spikes from dentils to left of date.

Obverse

Spike from dentils.

Reverse: Spikes from dentils near N and D in UNITED. Tool mark at right of I in UNITED. Depressions between OF and wing. Depression under 1 in ½, at bottom left of fraction diagonal.

Spikes from dentils near N and D in UNITED; tool mark at I.

Reverse

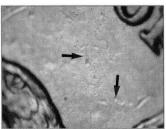

Depressions between OF and wing.

Depression under 1 in ½.

63

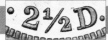

1906 Liberty Head $2.50 (Example 3)

Obverse: Tool marks at K-7 and K-12.

Obverse

Tool mark at K-7.

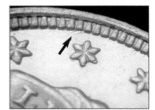

Tool mark at K-12.

Reverse: Tool mark (spike) near N in UNITED. Depression over eagle's left wing. Depression after last A in AMERICA. Broken D in denomination.

Reverse

Spike near N in UNITED.

Depression over eagle's left wing.

Depression after last A in AMERICA.

Broken D in 2½D.

1907 Liberty Head $2.50

Obverse: Tool mark from right of 7 in date.

Tool mark from right of 7 in date.

Obverse

Reverse: Tool marks through 2½. Raised blem below eagle's right wing. Doubled letters, with spike through top loop of R in AMERICA. Small raised pimples over AMERICA.

Tool marks through 2½.

Reverse

Blem below eagle's right wing.

Spike through top loop of R in AMERICA; surface pimples.

1908 Indian Head $2.50

Obverse: Weak/Fatty details. Large depression on jaw. Depressions on top portion of second feather from bottom. Depression between second and third stars on left.

Obverse

Depression on jaw.

Depressions on feather.

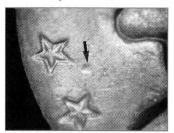

Depression between stars.

Reverse: Two depressions between eagle's wing and UNITED. Depression between L and A in DOLLAR. *Note:* This is a common false reverse die used on many other counterfeit Indian Head quarter eagles.

Reverse

Depressions near wing.

Depression between
L and A in DOLLAR.

1910 Indian Head $2.50

Obverse: Tool marks at back of neck. Depression in center of lowest feather. Depression to lower left of I in LIBERTY.

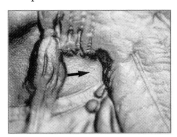

Tool marks at back of neck.

Obverse

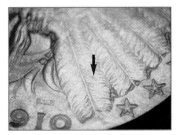

Depression in feather.

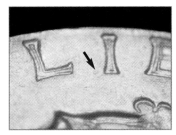

Depression near I in LIBERTY.

Reverse: Small spike from R, and depression under B, in PLURIBUS. Raised line through D in UNITED. Tool mark (raised line) through center of O in GOD.

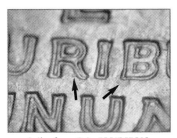

Spike from R in PLURIBUS;
depression under B.

Reverse

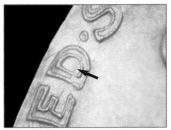

Line through D in UNITED.

Tool mark through O in GOD.

67

1911 Indian Head $2.50 (Example 1)

Obverse: Depressions on cheek.

Obverse

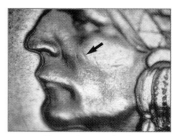

Depression on cheek.

Reverse: Depressions around LL in DOLLARS; in field above IN; and through second U in UNUM.

Reverse

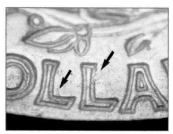

Depressions around
LL in DOLLARS.

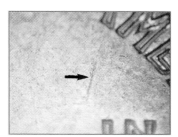

Depressions above IN.

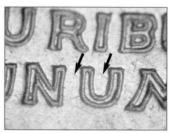

Depressions through
second U in UNUM.

1911 Indian Head $2.50 (Example 2)

Obverse: Blem on lower neck. Blem in front of throat. Blem above last 1 in date. Tool marks by sixth star on right.

Blems on and near lower neck.

Obverse

Blem above last 1 in date.

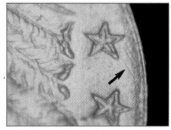

Tool marks by sixth star on right.

Reverse: Fine tool marks under R in PLURIBUS. Depression over second U in UNUM.

Tool marks under R in PLURIBUS; depression over UNUM.

Reverse

1911-D Indian Head $2.50 (Example 1)

Obverse: Tool marks ("worms") at back of neck (*Note:* remember to rotate the coin under a good light and view it at a severe angle to observe these and other diagnostics). Two small depressions below chin. Missing lowest point of sixth star on right.

Obverse

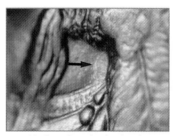

Tool marks at back of neck.

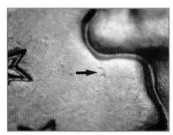

Small depressions below chin.

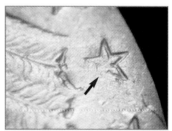

Missing point on sixth star on right.

Reverse: Depression in field above B in PLURIBUS. Depression between 2½ and D in DOLLARS.

Reverse

Depression above B in PLURIBUS.

Depression between
2½ and D in DOLLARS.

1911-D Indian Head $2.50 (Example 2)

Obverse: Two depressions in top feather. Depression in field between sixth and seventh stars on right. Two very shallow depressions under R in LIBERTY.

Depressions in feather; depression between stars.

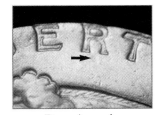

Depression under R in LIBERTY.

Obverse

Reverse: Depression under R in AMERICA. Tool marks through OD in GOD. Depression under U in TRUST. Incorrect style of D mintmark.

Depression under R in AMERICA.

Tool marks through OD in GOD.

Reverse

Depression under U in TRUST.

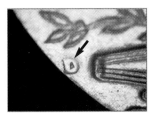

Incorrect style of D mintmark.

71

1911-D Indian Head $2.50 (Example 3)

Obverse: Tool marks at back of neck. Depression in front of nose.

Obverse

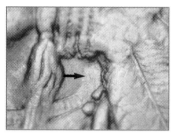

Tool marks at back of neck.

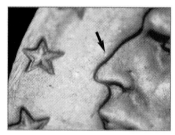

Depression in front of nose.

Reverse: Depressions between ½ and DOLLARS; to left of I in IN; and under last A in AMERICA.

Reverse

Depression in denomination.

Depression to left of I in IN.

Depression under
last A in AMERICA.

1912 Indian Head $2.50 (Example 1)

Obverse: Depression between feather end and fourth star on right. Depression in field below and to right of LIBERTY.

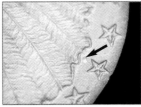

Depression near feather.

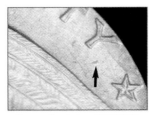

Depression below LIBERTY.

Obverse

Reverse: Long, thin, depressed groove running southwest from eagle's beak. Tool line between A and M in AMERICA. Line through G in GOD. Two grooves below E in AMERICA.

Groove running southwest from eagle's beak.

Tool line between A and M in AMERICA.

Reverse

Line through G in GOD.

Grooves below E in AMERICA.

1912 Indian Head $2.50 (Example 2)

Obverse: Depressions between 1 and 2 in date and to right of 2.

Obverse

Depressions around date.

Reverse: Depression midway between eagle and UNITED. Tool marks under N in UNUM.

Reverse

Depression between eagle and UNITED.

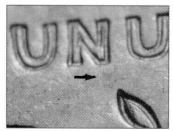

Tool marks under N in UNUM.

1913 Indian Head $2.50 (Example 1)

Obverse: Tool marks at back of neck. Depression under E in LIBERTY.

Tool marks at back of neck.

Obverse

Depression under E in LIBERTY.

Reverse: Depression under first A in AMERICA. Very light tool marks in same area.

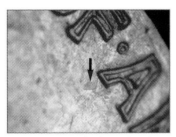

Depression and light tool marks
under first A in AMERICA.

Reverse

1913 Indian Head $2.50 (Example 2)

Obverse: All lettering and devices very bold and unlike a genuine coin. *Note:* Made from a hand-cut die.

Obverse

Detail of Indian Head portrait.

Reverse: All lettering and devices very bold and unlike a genuine coin. Note particularly E PLURIBUS UNUM and IN GOD WE TRUST. *Note:* Made from a hand-cut die.

Reverse

Detail of eagle and lettering.

Edge: Improper reeding.

Detail of eagle and lettering.

1914 Indian Head $2.50

Obverse: Depressions at rim over third star on right; on lower area of bust; and in field in front of bust. Depression in field under R in LIBERTY, over feather.

Depression over third star on right.

Obverse

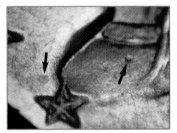

Depressions on and near bust.

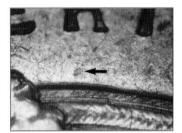

Depression under R in LIBERTY.

Reverse: Depressions through second U in UNUM and at first T in TRUST.

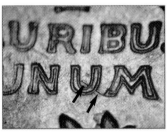

Depression through
second U in UNUM.

Reverse

Depression at first T in TRUST.

1914-D Indian Head $2.50 (Example 1)

Obverse: Depression on bust, below necklace. Depression at top point of third star on right. Small depression on slanting side of 4 in date, near B.L.P. Small depression above and to right of crescent in row of blossoms in headdress.

Obverse

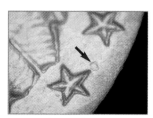

Depression on
bust, below necklace.

Depression at
third star on right.

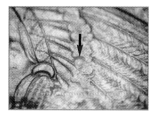

Depression at 4 in date.

Depression in headdress.

Reverse: Raised spikes at top left and bottom left of L in PLURIBUS. Soft, mushy D mintmark. Depression to left of eagle's claw.

Reverse

Spikes at L in PLURIBUS.

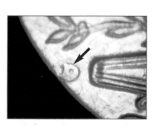

Soft, mushy D mintmark.

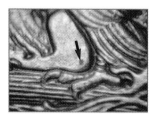

Depression to
left of eagle's claw.

HISTORY OF THE UNITED STATES MINT —— AND ITS COINAGE ——

From its roots in the pre-colonial and colonial eras, through independence and confederation, the intrigues, tribulations, and triumphs of the 1800s, and into the modern day—through war, peace, famine, earthquakes, gold rushes, good times and bad—*History of the United States Mint and Its Coinage* follows the twists and turns of one of the federal government's most intriguing bureaus.

Every major U.S. mint is described in detail: Philadelphia, Denver, and New Orleans; as well as the branch mints of Charlotte, Dahlonega, Carson City, and West Point— and even the mint set up in Manila, in the Philippines, by the U.S. government. Along the way we learn about the California Gold Rush, the Civil War and its effect on America's economy, the fierce battles of silver vs. gold, how world events affected U.S. coins, and more.

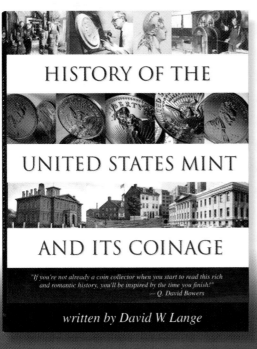

- Historical, technical, and artistic details of the Mint and its coins

- Vintage photographs and documents throughout

- Hundreds of enlarged, high-detail images of American coins, tokens, and medals

- Special "Mint Topics" on 1964 silver dollars, bullion coins, state quarters, new nickels, and more

1915 Indian Head $2.50 (Example 1)

Obverse: Large depression to right of 5 in date, near lowest feather.

Obverse

Depression near 5 in date.

Reverse: Depressions by top left leaf; above ½ in denomination; and between L and A in DOLLARS.

Reverse

Depression by top left leaf.

Depression above
½ in denomination.

Depression between
L and A in DOLLARS.

1915 Indian Head $2.50 (Example 2)

Obverse: Depressions in field in front of lips, jaw, and throat.

Depression in front of lips.

Obverse

Depressions in front
of jaw and throat.

Reverse: Depression in front of eagle's right leg.

Depression in front of leg.

Reverse

1925-D Indian Head $2.50 (Example 1)

Obverse: Tool marks on neck, above first star on left. Tool marks in front of eye. Depressions on cheekbone.

Obverse

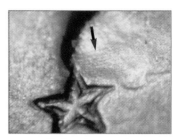

Tool marks on neck.

Tool marks in front of eye.

Depressions on cheekbone.

Reverse: Three depressions in field to left of IN. Depressed groove through LA in DOLLARS.

Reverse

Depressions to left of IN.

Groove through LA in DOLLARS.

1925-D Indian Head $2.50 (Example 2)

Obverse: Depressions on top portion of third feather from bottom, and above top feather over head (below RT in LIBERTY). Depressions just above headband. Points of stars 3, 4, and 5 (on left) falling off rim of coin.

Depression on feather.

Obverse

Depressions just above
headband and above top feather.

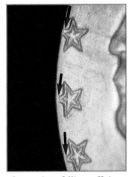

Star points falling off rim.

Reverse: Depression below GO in GOD. Depression above D in DOLLARS.

Depression below GO in GOD.

Reverse

Depression above D in DOLLARS.

1925-D Indian Head $2.50 (Example 3)

Obverse: Short outer point to star in front of nose. Depression to left of B in LIBERTY ("Broken B"). Depressions behind nose and on jaw.

Obverse

Short outer point to star.

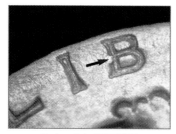

Broken B in LIBERTY.

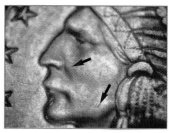

Depressions behind nose and on jaw.

Reverse: Depression between P and L in PLURIBUS. Depression through D in GOD; blem next to it. Long, raised line from first T in TRUST, stretching up to last A in AMERICA.

Reverse

Depression between
P and L in PLURIBUS.

Depression and blem at
D in GOD; long, raised line.

1925-D Indian Head $2.50 (Example 4)

Obverse: Tool marks at back of neck and heavier ones in front of throat.

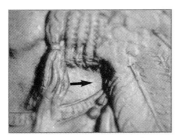

Tool marks at back of neck.

Obverse

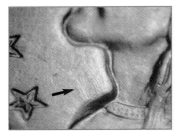

Tool marks in front of throat.

Reverse: Depressions in front of and between eagle's legs.

Depressions in front of eagle's leg.

Reverse

Depression between eagle's legs.

1927 Indian Head $2.50

Obverse: Color off, and design elements different from an authentic coin. *Note:* Struck from a hand-cut die.

Obverse

Detail of Indian Head portrait.

Reverse: Color off, and design elements different from an authentic coin. *Note:* Struck from a hand-cut die.

Reverse

Detail of eagle and lettering.

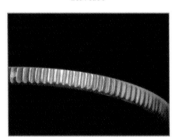

Edge: Coarse reeding.

1928 Indian Head $2.50 (Example 1)

Obverse: Depression between third and fourth stars on left, with raised blem adjacent to it. Small depression between second and third stars on right.

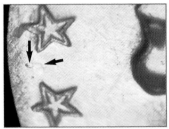

Depression and blem between third and fourth start on left.

Obverse

Depression between second and third stars on right.

Reverse: Depressed groove running left from eagle's neck. Small depression and tool marks in field between eagle's wing and ED in UNITED. Groove running from D in DOLLARS to leaf above.

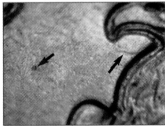

Depressed groove running left from eagle's neck; depression and tool marks in field.

Reverse

Groove running from D in DOLLARS to leaf above.

1928 Indian Head $2.50 (Example 2)

Obverse: Raised lump in lower loop of 8 in date. Large groove on each side of top of 2 in date. Depression between Y in LIBERTY and star. Tool marks ("worms") at back of neck. Depressed groove connecting third and fourth stars on left. Raised diagonal line in center of third feather from bottom.

Obverse

Blems in date.

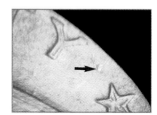

Depression between
Y in LIBERTY and star.

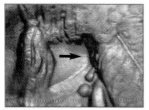

Tool marks at back of neck.

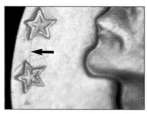

Groove connecting third
and fourth stars on left.

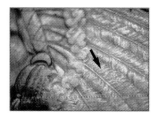

Line in center of third
feather from bottom.

Reverse: Two depressions above R in DOLLARS. Depression through top of 2 in ½. Three depressions in field to left of eagle's wing, under TE in UNITED. Small depressions over eagle's beak and behind neck.

Reverse

Depressions above
R in DOLLARS.

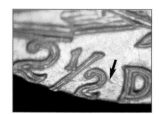

Depression through
top of 2 in ½.

Depressions in field
to left of eagle's wing.

Depressions over eagle's
beak and behind neck.

1928 Indian Head $2.50 (Example 3)

Obverse: Depression between third and fourth stars on left, with raised blem beside it. Blem between T and Y in LIBERTY, and a very shallow depression below it.

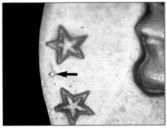

Depression between stars, with raised blem beside it.

Obverse

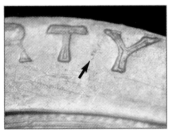

Blem and depression between T and Y in LIBERTY.

Reverse: Heavy, raised tool marks in and around 2½. Depression above I in PLURIBUS. Depression in field between eagle's wing and ED in UNITED.

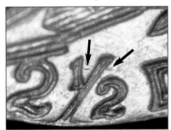

Tool marks in and around 2½.

Reverse

Depression above I in PLURIBUS.

Depression in field between eagle's wing and ED in UNITED.

89

1929 Indian Head $2.50 (Example 1)

Obverse: Roughness at back of neck (this normally would be tooled away by a counterfeiter).

Obverse

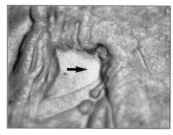

Roughness at back of neck.

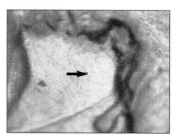

Closeup of roughness.

Reverse: Depression through RIB of PLURIBUS.

Reverse

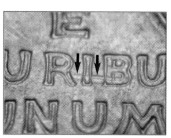

Depression through
RIB of PLURIBUS.

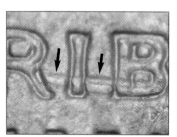

Closeup of depression.

1929 Indian Head $2.50 (Example 2)

Obverse: Tool marks ("worms") at neck. Depressions in front of nose and below neck.

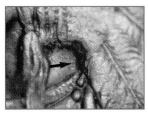

Tool marks at neck.

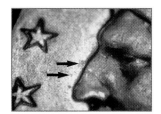

Depressions in front of nose.

Obverse

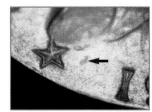

Depressions below neck.

Reverse: Depressions below U in UNITED; between eagle's legs; and under BU of PLURIBUS. Tool marks under right side of N in UNUM.

Depression below
U in UNITED.

Depressions between
eagle's legs.

Reverse

Depression under
BU of PLURIBUS.

Tool marks under right
side of N in UNUM.

91

1929 Indian Head $2.50 (Example 3)

Obverse: Tool marks at back of neck. (*Note:* Tilt to see clearly.) Depression at bottom of B in LIBERTY. Two long, thin, raised parallel lines from 9 in date up through bottoms of feathers to second star on right.

Obverse

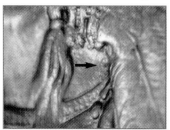

Tool marks at back of neck.

Depression at bottom of B in LIBERTY.

Lines from 9 in date to second star on right.

Reverse: Depression in field above ½ in denomination, under arrow shafts. Small depression in field between wing and ED of UNITED. Several parallel grooves at lower part of S in PLURIBUS.

Reverse

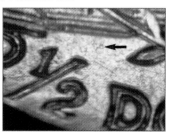

Depression above ½ in denomination.

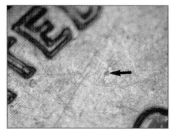

Depression in field between wing and ED of UNITED.

Parallel grooves at lower part of S in PLURIBUS.

$3 Gold Pieces

Be sure to read the Rules of Thumb on pages 1–9. They contain general guidelines relevant to the study of every counterfeit United States $3 gold piece.

You should be aware that many other counterfeit gold coins exist in the market than those covered in this book. The nearly 200 examples described here will educate you on what to look for, but be forewarned that no book will ever be able to illustrate *every* counterfeit.

1854 Indian Princess Head $3

Obverse: Weak/Fatty details. Spike above second T in STATES. Depression to lower left of E in STATES. Blem (raised lump) in center of feathers in headdress.

Obverse

Spike above second T in STATES; depression to lower left of E.

Blem in headdress.

Reverse: Rim spikes from K-11 to leaf and below to northeast. Spikes at K-3 and K-7.

Reverse

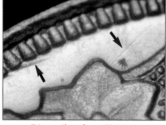

Rim spikes from K-11 to leaf and below to northeast.

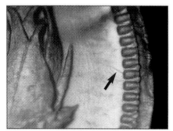

Spike at K-3.

Spike at K-7.

1855 Indian Princess Head $3 (Example 1)

Obverse: Spikes from upper serif of first S in STATES; from dentils over A and E in STATES; over F in OF; over M in AMERICA; and between C and A in AMERICA.

Spike from first S in STATES.

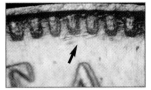

Spikes from dentils over A in STATES.

Obverse

Spikes from dentils over E in STATES.

Spikes over F in OF.

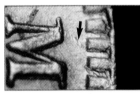

Spikes from dentils over M in AMERICA.

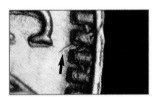

Spikes from dentils over C in AMERICA.

Reverse: Depressions in field to left and upper right of 3 in denomination. Spikes from topmost left thin leaf and broad leaf next to it. Spikes in field near dentils at K-8 and under blossoms to its right.

Depressions around 3 in denomination.

Spikes from leaves.

Reverse

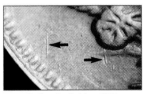

Spikes in field at K-8.

1855 Indian Princess Head $3 (Example 2)

Obverse: Spikes from dentils over D in UNITED. Weak/Fatty (mushy) letters. "Doubled-die" letters. *Note:* This is a common false obverse die used on several other counterfeit $3 gold pieces (see also 1867).

Obverse

Spikes over D in UNITED; mushy letters.

Mushy and "doubled-die" letters in UNITED.

Reverse: Weak/Fatty devices. Doubled date, especially visible on first 5 in date. Tool marks through dentils at K-12. Raised blem in field at K-8½. Tool marks (spikes) from many dentils.

Reverse

Doubled date.

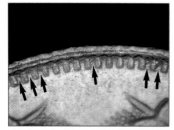

Tool marks through dentils at K-12.

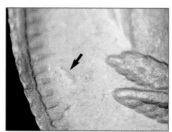

Blem in field at K-8½.

1855 Indian Princess Head $3 (Example 3)

Obverse: Weak/Fatty (very mushy, indistinct) letters, etc. Raised blems all over obverse, especially through AMERICA. Long die crack to left of AMERICA. "Surface doubling" on many letters. Tool marks on throat and under OF. Unusually sharp rim.

Long die crack to left of AMERICA; unusually sharp rim; blems through AMERICA.

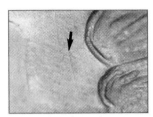

Tool marks on throat.

Obverse

Tool marks under OF.

Reverse: Weak/Fatty details. Raised blems all over reverse. Tool marks (spikes) at K-3 and K-9; on bow knot; and to right of right ribbon end in field.

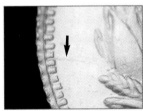

Tool marks at K-9.

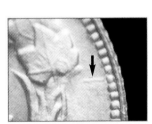

Tool marks at K-3.

Reverse

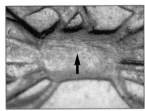

Tool marks on bow knot.

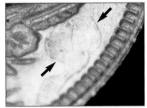

Tool marks to right of ribbon end.

1857 Indian Princess Head $3

Obverse: Broken upper left serif on I in UNITED and in AMERICA. (*Note:* The broken serif is found on some genuine 1857 $3 gold pieces as well.) Thin, straightlines through AME in AMERICA. Series of tool marks between tip of chin and UN (in UNITED) and on throat.

Obverse

Broken serif on I in UNITED.

Broken serif on I in AMERICA.

Lines through
AME in AMERICA.

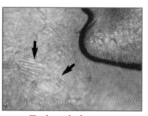

Tool marks between
chin and UN in UNITED.

Tool marks on throat.

Reverse: Depressions in center of lowest broad leaf on left. Depressions in field between leaves and rim at K-2.

Reverse

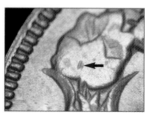

Depressions on lowest
broad leaf on left.

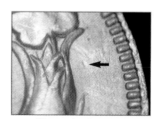

Depression between
leaves and rim at K-2.

1867 Indian Princess Head $3

Obverse: Weak/Fatty (mushy) letters. "Doubled-die" letters on obverse. *Note:* This is a common false obverse die used on several other counterfeit $3 gold pieces (see also 1855 Example 2).

Mushy and "doubled-die"
letters in UNITED.

Obverse

Closeup of doubling.

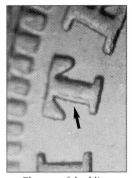

Closeup of doubling.

Reverse: No distinguishing counterfeit diagnostics.

1874 Indian Princess Head $3 (Example 1)

Obverse: Weak/Fatty details. Depression between T and E in UNITED. Depression in field below chin. Letters in OF AMERICA much weaker than in UNITED STATES.

Obverse

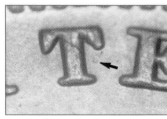

Depression between
T and E in UNITED.

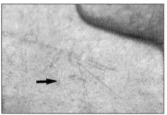

Depression in field below chin.

Reverse: Several blems in field at K-7 between leaves and rim, and also below bow. Two spikes in dentil below left ribbon end. Large depression below 1 in date. Blem on upper left loop of 8 in date. Depression on second L in DOLLARS. *Note:* This is a common false reverse die used on other counterfeit $3 gold pieces (see also 1874 Examples 2 and 3).

Reverse

Blems and spikes at K-7.

Depression below 1,
and blem on 8, in date.

Depression on second
L in DOLLARS.

1874 Indian Princess Head $3 (Example 2)

Obverse: Weak/Fatty details. Blem in field between OF and AMERICA.

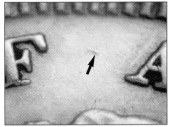

Blem between OF and AMERICA.

Obverse

Reverse: Several blems in field at K-7 between leaves and rim, and also below bow. Blem on upper left loop of 8 in date. Depression on second L in DOLLARS. *Note:* This is a common false reverse die used on other counterfeit $3 gold pieces (see also 1874 Examples 1 and 3).

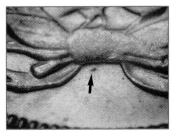

Blem below bow.

Reverse

Blem at K-7.

Blem on 8 in date.

1874 Indian Princess Head $3 (Example 3)

Obverse: Weak/Fatty details. Depressions between and underneath T, E, and D in UNITED. Blems behind eye and on lower neck. Large diagonal groove between I and B in LIBERTY. Depression in field in front of throat.

Obverse

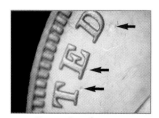

Depressions between and underneath T and E in UNITED.

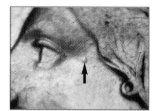

Blem behind eye.

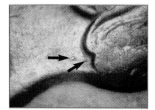

Blems on lower neck.

Groove between I and B in LIBERTY.

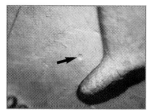

Depression in front of throat.

Reverse: Several blems in field at K-7, between leaves and rim below bow. Blem on upper left loop of 8 in date. Depression on second L in DOLLARS. *Note:* This is a common false reverse die used on other counterfeit $3 gold pieces (see also 1874 Examples 1 and 2).

Reverse

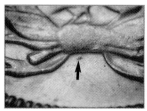

Blem below bow.

Blem on 8 in date.

Blem at K-7.

1878 Indian Princess Head $3 (Example 1)

Obverse: Weak/Fatty (soft, mushy) details. Depression between E and R and "bumps" on tops of R, I, and C in AMERICA. Two thin spikes from dentil at upper left of O in OF.

Depression and "bumps" in AMERICA.

Obverse

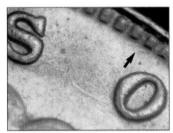

Spikes from dentil near O in OF.

Reverse: Weak/Fatty features, especially in central area. Depression in top of second L in DOLLARS. Second 8 much stronger than 187 in date.

Mushy letters on reverse; depression in first L in DOLLARS; strong second 8.

1878 Indian Princess Head $3 (Example 2)

Obverse: Weak/Fatty details. Depressions below D in UNITED and on upper and lower serifs of E in STATES.

Obverse

Depression below D in UNITED.

Depressions on E in STATES.

Reverse: Weak/Fatty details. Weak 187 and strong 8 in date. Weak, thin wreath stalk under D of DOLLAR. No die polish in center of bow, which is usually seen on most genuine coins. Depression on right bow loop.

Reverse

Weak 187 and strong 8 in date.

Weak, thin wreath stalk
under D of DOLLAR.

Depression on right bow loop.

1878 Indian Princess Head $3 (Example 3)

Obverse: Weak/Fatty letters and devices. Depression in field after last S in STATES. Raised blems behind eye and on lower neck.

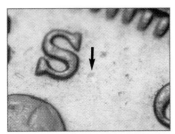

Depression after last S in STATES.

Obverse

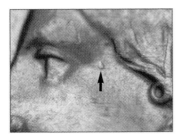

Blem behind eye.

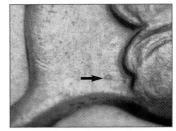

Blem on lower neck.

Reverse: Very fine circular tool line all around circumference, between dentils and letters. Granular surface at K-6, under bow.

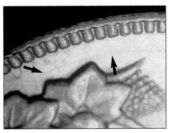

Circular tool line
around circumference.

Reverse

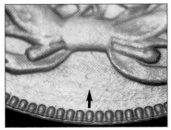

Granular surface under bow.

105

1882 Indian Princess Head $3 (Example 1)

Obverse: Weak/Fatty details (lettering, etc.).

Obverse

Mushy letters.

Mushy letters.

Reverse: Depressions in field to left of date; above 2 in date; and on second L in DOLLARS.

Reverse

Depression above 2 in date.

Depression to left of date.

Depression on second
L in DOLLARS.

1882 Indian Princess Head $3 (Example 2)

Obverse: Weak/Fatty details. Spikes in dentils and through second T in STATES. Spike from dentil near last A in AMERICA; long, depressed line near ERICA.

Spikes in dentils and through second T in STATES.

Obverse

Spike from dentil near last A in AMERICA.

Line near ERICA in AMERICA.

Reverse: Small blems above and to upper right of 2 in date. Spike on outer top left part of 3 in denomination, and depression in upper ball of 3. Depressions on left and right bow loops.

Blems above and to upper right of 2 in date.

Reverse

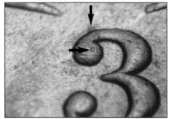

Spike and depression on 3 in denomination.

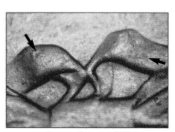

Depressions on left and right bow loops.

107

1882 Indian Princess Head $3 (Example 3)

Note: This is the most heavily counterfeited date for $3 gold pieces. "I would estimate that 90% of the gold pieces ANACS examines are counterfeit" (Randy Campbell, ANACS professional grader).

Obverse: "Omega" counterfeit; note Ω design inside R of LIBERTY.

Obverse

Omega inside R of LIBERTY.

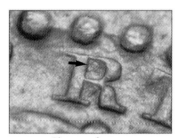

Closeup of omega.

Reverse: Doubled 2 in date, with loss of detail from the doubling usually seen on genuine coins of this date.

Reverse

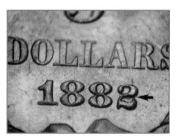

Doubled 2 in date.

Closeup of doubled 2.

Half Eagles

Be sure to read the Rules of Thumb on pages 1–9. They contain general guidelines relevant to the study of every counterfeit United States half eagle.

You should be aware that many other counterfeit gold coins exist in the market than those covered in this book. The nearly 200 examples described here will educate you on what to look for, but be forewarned that no book will ever be able to illustrate *every* counterfeit.

1811 Capped Bust $5

Obverse: "Sunken" (concave) dentils and centers of numbers in date. Two depressions in dentils over cap. Long depression below ear. Blem (raised lump) on jaw. Depression in hair curl, above clasp. Blem under point of hair curl.

Obverse

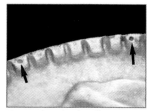

"Sunken" dentils and numbers in date.

Depressions in dentils over cap.

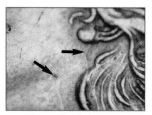

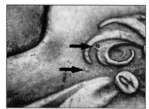

Depression below ear; blem on jaw.

Depression and blem in hair.

Reverse: "Sunken" (concave) letters in legends. C in AMERICA doubled at base, as seen on genuine coins struck from the original die.

Reverse

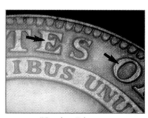

"Sunken" letters.

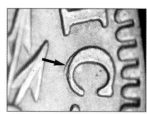

Doubled C in AMERICA.

1881-CC Liberty Head, With Motto $5

Obverse: Depressions on cheek; in field in front of chin; and on nose and neck. Fine, raised tool lines throughout entire obverse field.

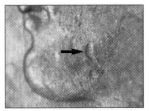

Depression on cheek.

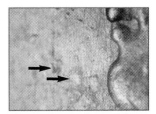

Depressions in front of chin.

Obverse

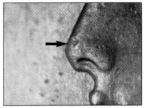

Depression on nose.

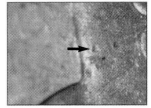

Depression on neck.

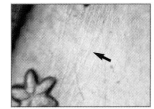

Tool lines throughout field.

Reverse: Depression to left of CC mintmark. Depression under E of WE in motto. Depressions under M in AMERICA and in field between wing and ED in UNITED. Depressions in center of both dots on each side of FIVE D.

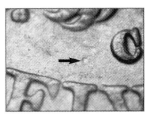

Depression to left of CC mintmark.

Depression under E of WE.

Reverse

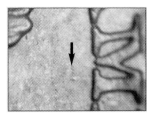

Depression under M in AMERICA.

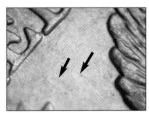

Depressions between wing and ED in UNITED.

111

1882 Liberty Head, With Motto $5

Obverse: Tool mark under 1 in date. Raised blems in field in front of face. Long tool mark in field under bun.

Obverse

Tool mark under 1 in date.

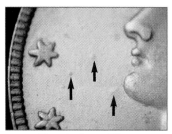

Blems in front of face.

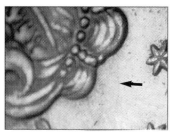

Tool mark in field under bun.

Reverse: Tool marks at RI in AMERICA; under F in FIVE; and between eagle's left wing and scroll. Tool marks through many dentils.

Reverse

Tool marks at RI in AMERICA.

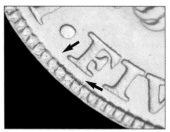

Tool marks under F in FIVE.

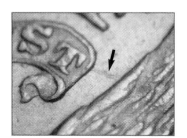

Tool mark between
eagle's wing and scroll.

1885 Liberty Head, With Motto $5

Obverse: Depressions on cheek and by eye. Two depressions on neck.

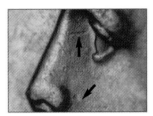

Depressions on
cheek and by eye.

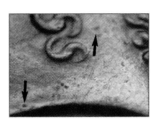

Depressions on neck.

Obverse

Reverse: Spikes from dentils at AMERICA and at I in UNITED; under F in FIVE;
and over first S in STATES.

Spikes from dentils
at AMERICA.

Spike from dentil
at I in UNITED.

Reverse

Spike from dentil
under F in FIVE.

Spike from dentil
over first S in STATES.

1887-S Liberty Head, With Motto $5

Obverse: Weak/Fatty details. Very rough surface on entire obverse. Curved, raised line from center of second 8 in date, down to bottom of 7. Doubled nose and base of bust. Large blem above bun, above fourth star on right.

Obverse

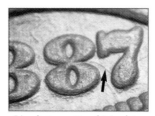

Line between 8 and 7 in date.

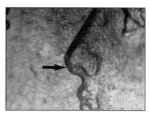

Doubled nose.

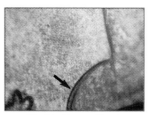

Doubled base of bust.

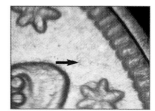

Blem above bun.

Reverse: Many small raised blems to right of eagle's head. Curved, raised line below eagle's left wing, running into field. *Note:* This is a common false reverse die used on many other counterfeit S-mint Liberty Head half eagles (see also 1906-S).

Reverse

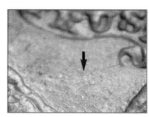

Blems to right of eagle's head.

Line below eagle's left wing.

1891-CC Liberty Head, With Motto $5

Obverse: Weak/Fatty details. "Wavy" depressions behind 189 in date. Depressions by fifth star on left and in field behind neck.

Depressions behind 189 in date.

Obverse

Depression by fifth star on left.

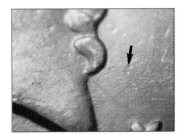

Depression behind neck.

Reverse: Depressions to left of CC mintmark, and in field to right of eagle's left wing. *Note:* This is another common false reverse die used on many counterfeit Carson City Mint Liberty Head half eagle gold pieces.

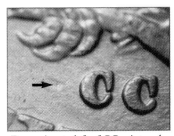

Depression to left of CC mintmark.

Reverse

Depression to right of eagle's wing.

1892 Liberty Head, With Motto $5

Obverse: Depressions in field in front of chin; on cheek; and on jaw.

Obverse

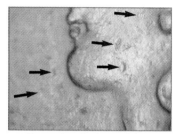

Depressions in front of chin;
on cheek; and on jaw.

Reverse: Blem above E in FIVE. Depression under M in AMERICA. Spikes at K-10½, above eagle's wing tip.

Reverse

Blem above E in FIVE.

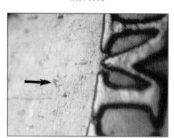

Depression under M in AMERICA.

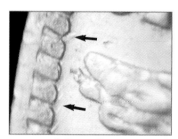

Spikes at K-10½.

1892-CC Liberty Head, With Motto $5

Obverse: Weak/Fatty details. Fine, raised lines in fields throughout. Depressions on chin and jaw and on center of bust below lowest hair curl.

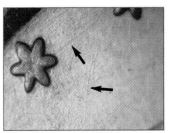

Lines in field.

Obverse

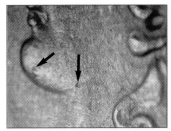

Depressions on chin and jaw.

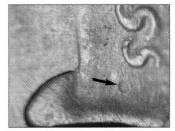

Depression on bust.

Reverse: Depressions to left of CC mintmark; above right dot; and after second A in AMERICA. Large depression behind eagle's head. *Note:* This is another common false reverse die used on many counterfeit Liberty Head half eagle gold pieces (see also 1893-CC).

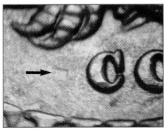

Depression to left of CC mintmark.

Reverse

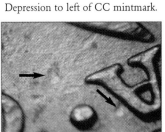

Depressions above right dot and after second A in AMERICA.

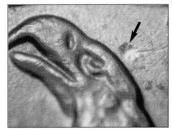

Depression behind eagle's head.

117

1893-CC Liberty Head, With Motto $5

Obverse: Raised blems all around date, most stars, tiara and bun. Depressions below chin and eye; on nose; and in front of face. Date doubled to left.

Obverse

Doubled numbers;
blems around date.

Blems around stars and tiara.

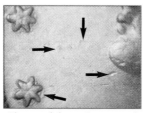

Blems and depressions around
stars; in field; and below chin.

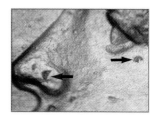

Depressions on
nose and below eye.

Reverse: Depressions to left of CC mintmark; above right dot; and after second A in AMERICA. Large depression behind eagle's head. *Note:* This is a common false reverse die used on many counterfeit Liberty Head half eagle gold pieces (see also 1892-CC).

Reverse

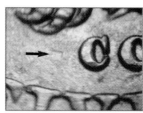

Depression to left
of CC mintmark.

Depressions above right dot and
after second A in AMERICA.

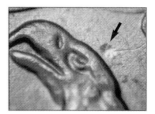

Depression behind eagle's head.

1899 Liberty Head, With Motto $5

Obverse: Fine, raised lines covering entire obverse field, especially around date. Depression on lower jaw. Small spike over star at K-1½.

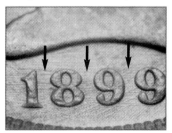

Lines around date.

Obverse

Depression on jaw.

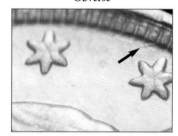

Spike at K-1½.

Reverse: Blems all over eagle's left wing, near neck. Fine, raised lines running from OF through wing, to rim at first A in AMERICA. Tool lines above CA. Tool lines also through and above UNITE in UNITED. *Note:* This is yet another common false reverse die used on many counterfeit Liberty Head half eagle gold pieces (see also 1900 Examples 1 and 2, and 1908 Example 2).

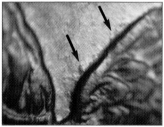

Blems at eagle's left wing.

Reverse

Lines running from OF to rim.

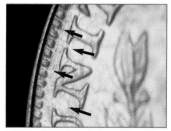

Lines through and above UNITE.

1900 Liberty Head, With Motto $5 (Example 1)

Obverse: Spike from dentils above Liberty's head.

Obverse

Spike from dentils
above Liberty's head.

Reverse: Blems all over eagle's left wing, near neck. Fine, raised lines leading from OF through wing, to rim at first A in AMERICA. Tool lines above CA. Tool lines through and above UNITE in UNITED. *Note:* This is a common false reverse die used on many counterfeit Liberty Head half eagle gold pieces (see also 1899, 1900 Example 2, and 1908 Example 2).

Reverse

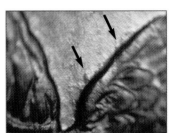

Blems at eagle's left wing.

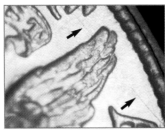

Lines running from OF to rim.

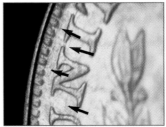

Lines through and above
UNITE in UNITED.

1900 Liberty Head, With Motto $5 (Example 2)

Obverse: Weak/Fatty details. Large blems below bust (over first 0 in date); near dentils to right of date; and near first star. Blems also behind lower bust and attached to right center of 1 in date.

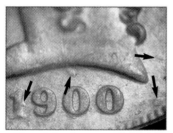

Blems below bust; near dentils to right of date; and near first star.

Obverse

Reverse: Blems all over eagle's left wing, near neck. Fine, raised lines leading from OF through wing, to above first A in AMERICA and above CA. Tool lines also through and above UNITE in UNITED. *Note:* This is a common false reverse die used on many counterfeit Liberty Head half eagle gold pieces (see also 1899, 1900 Example 1, and 1908 Example 2).

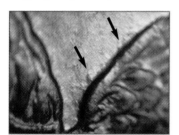

Blems at eagle's left wing.

Reverse

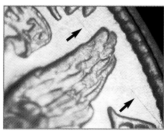

Lines running from OF to rim.

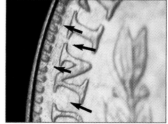

Lines through and above UNITE.

121

1906-S Liberty Head, With Motto $5

Obverse: Weak/Fatty details. Doubled lower bust and nostril. Small blem above 9 in date. Tool marks around lower right stars.

Obverse

Blem above 9 in date; doubled bust.

Doubled nostril.

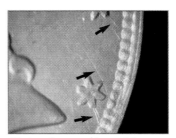

Tool marks around lower right stars.

Reverse: Many small raised blems to right of eagle's head. Curved, raised line below eagle's left wing, running into field. *Note:* This is a common false reverse die used on many counterfeit S-mint Liberty Head half eagles (see also 1887-S).

Reverse

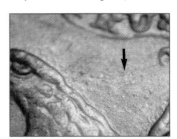

Blems to right of eagle's head.

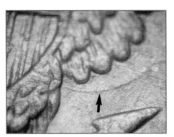

Line below eagle's left wing.

1908 Liberty Head, With Motto $5 (Example 1)

Obverse: Weak/Fatty details. Many small, raised blems on cheek and jaw. Spike from top of head.

Blems on cheek and jaw.

Obverse

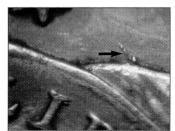

Spike from top of head.

Reverse: Depression in field under eagle's beak. Depression between eagle's left wing and AMER in AMERICA.

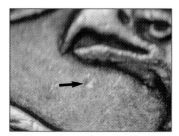

Depression under eagle's beak.

Reverse

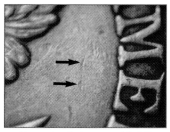

Depression between eagle's left wing and AMER in AMERICA.

123

1908 Liberty Head, With Motto $5 (Example 2)

Obverse: Small blems throughout date area, especially in top loops of 0 and 8. Raised blems below ear; on cheek; and on neck, to upper right of dangling hair curl.

Obverse

Blems throughout date.

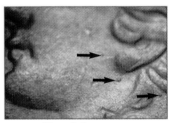

Blems below ear; on cheek; and on neck.

Reverse: Blems all over eagle's left wing, near neck. Fine, raised lines leading from OF through wing, to rim at first A in AMERICA. Tool lines above CA. Tool lines through and above UNITE in UNITED. *Note:* This is a common false reverse die used on many counterfeit Liberty Head half eagles (see also 1899 and 1900 Examples 1 and 2).

Reverse

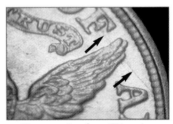

Lines running from OF to rim.

Lines through and above UNITE in UNITED.

1908 Indian Head $5

Obverse: Tool marks at back of neck.

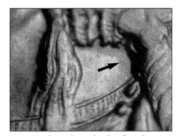

Tool marks at back of neck.

Obverse

Reverse: Depressions in field to left of E in E PLURIBUS UNUM; above V in FIVE; and above eagle's head.

Depression to left of E in
E PLURIBUS UNUM.

Reverse

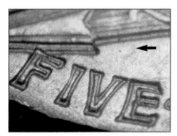

Depression above V in FIVE.

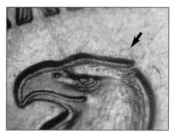

Depression above eagle's head.

1908-D Indian Head $5

Obverse: Tool marks at back of neck. Depression in field to right of B.L.P. Tool marks in depressed area around chin.

Obverse

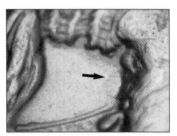

Tool marks at back of neck.

Depression to right of B.L.P.

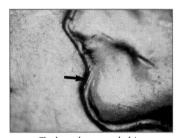

Tool marks around chin.

Reverse: No distinguishing counterfeit diagnostics.

1909 Indian Head $5 (Example 1)

Obverse: Depressions on cheek and jaw. Depression under jaw. Tool marks at back of neck. Depression between fourth and fifth stars on right.

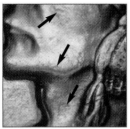

Depressions on cheek and jaw;
depression under jaw.

Obverse

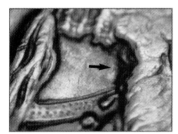

Tool marks at back of neck.

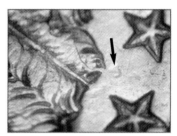

Depression between fourth
and fifth stars on right.

Reverse: Depression in field above D in DOLLARS, at leaf tip. Depression above S in PLURIBUS, next to eagle's breast.

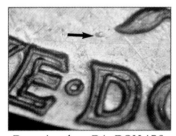

Depression above D in DOLLARS.

Reverse

Depression above S in PLURIBUS.

1909 Indian Head $5 (Example 2)

Obverse: Depressions in field below RT of LIBERTY and between third and fourth stars on right. Depressions in third and fourth feathers from bottom, and to right of first star on left.

Obverse

Two depressions in field below RT of LIBERTY.

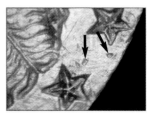

Depressions between third and fourth stars on right.

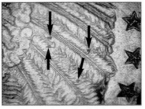

Depressions in third and fourth feathers from bottom.

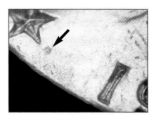

Depression to right of first star on left.

Reverse: Huge depression to upper left of E in E PLURIBUS UNUM. Die cracks from arrow points to rim left of leaves, and through AT in STATES. Tool marks under arrow shafts, above D in DOLLARS.

Reverse

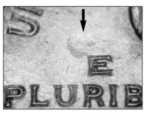

Depression to left of E in E PLURIBUS UNUM.

Die crack from arrow points to rim left of leaves.

Die crack through AT in STATES.

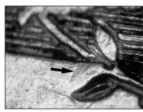

Tool marks under arrow shafts.

1909-D Indian Head $5

Obverse: Tool marks ("worms") at back of neck. Depression between fourth and fifth stars on right. Depression between sixth star on left and L of LIBERTY. Spikes running from fifth and sixth stars on right toward feathers.

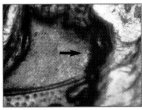

Tool marks at back of neck.

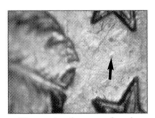

Depression between fourth and fifth stars on right.

Obverse

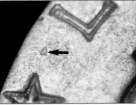

Depression between sixth star on left and L of LIBERTY.

Spikes running from fifth and sixth stars on right toward feathers.

Reverse: Broken bottom of U in UNITED. Depressions in center of, and above, arrow points; and through S in PLURIBUS.

Broken U in UNITED.

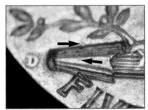

Depressions in center of, and above, arrow points.

Reverse

Depression through S in PLURIBUS.

1909-S Indian Head $5

Obverse: Tool marks at back of neck.

Tool marks at back of neck.

Obverse

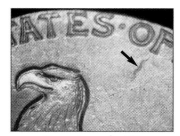

Closeup of tool marks.

Reverse: Long depression in field under OF. Wrong S mintmark ("wormy", with diagonal serifs).

Depression under OF.

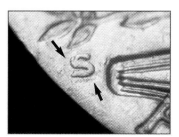

Reverse

Wrong S mintmark.

1910-D Indian Head $5

Obverse: Depression at rim after L in LIBERTY. Depression in field between second star on left and throat.

Obverse

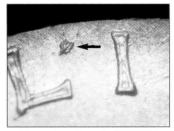

Depression after L in LIBERTY.

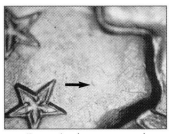

Depression between second star on left and throat.

Reverse: Depression in field to left of eagle's beak. Depressions to left of IN.

Reverse

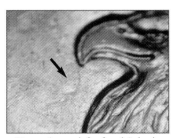

Depression to left of eagle's beak.

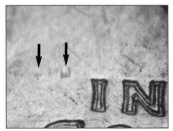

Depressions to left of IN.

1911 Indian Head $5

Obverse: Date runs off edge of coin. B.L.P. is too well defined. Tool marks at back of neck. Depression between third and fourth stars on right.

Date runs off edge of coin; B.L.P. is too well defined.

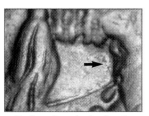

Tool marks at back of neck.

Obverse

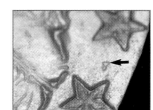

Depression between third and fourth stars on right.

Reverse: Depression in field between wing and UNITED. Large depression between eagle's legs. Depressions to left of first U in UNUM, and at rim to left of F in FIVE.

Depression between wing and UNITED.

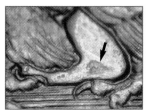

Depression between eagle's legs.

Reverse

Depression to left of first U in UNUM.

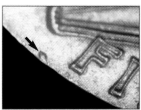

Depression to left of F in FIVE.

1912 Indian Head $5

Obverse: Depressions above B.L.P. and on cheek.

Obverse

Depressions above B.L.P.

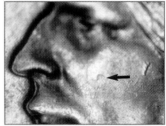

Depression on cheek.

Reverse: Depressions between eagle's leg and M of UNUM; above US in PLURIBUS; and in field above E D of FIVE DOLLARS.

Reverse

Depressions at eagle's leg and above US in PLURIBUS.

Depression in field above E D of FIVE DOLLARS.

1912-S Indian Head $5

Obverse: Huge depression above eye, with two tool marks to right. (*Note:* this is a strike-through error from the counterfeiter's minting.) Depression by Y in LIBERTY. Stubby star points on first two stars on right.

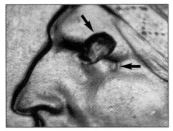

Depression above eye,
with tool marks to right.

Obverse

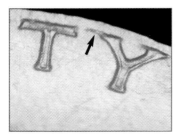

Depression by Y in LIBERTY.

Stubby star points.

Reverse: Wrong S mintmark ("wormy," with diagonal serifs), with tool marks surrounding.

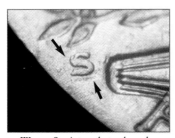

Wrong S mintmark; tool marks.

Reverse

135

1913 Indian Head $5

Obverse: Tool mark to left of R in LIBERTY.

Obverse

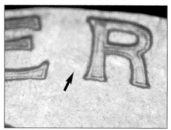

Tool mark to left of R in LIBERTY.

Reverse: Tool marks above U in PLURIBUS. Depressions to left of eagle's leg and to left of E in E PLURIBUS UNUM.

Reverse

Tool marks above U in PLURIBUS; depression to left of E in E PLURIBUS UNUM.

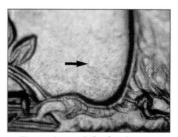

Depression to left of eagle's leg.

1915 Indian Head $5

Obverse: Depression on bottom of long, curved design element above B.L.P. Depressions below R in LIBERTY and on jaw.

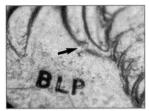

Depression on curved design element above B.L.P.

Depression below R in LIBERTY.

Obverse

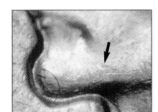

Depression on jaw.

Reverse: Two raised blems between arrow points and leaf above. Depression in field to left of eagle's right leg. Raised blems around IB in PLURIBUS. Depressions below eagle's claw, in arrow shafts.

Raised blems between arrow points and leaf above.

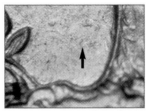

Depression to left of eagle's right leg.

Reverse

Raised blems around IB in PLURIBUS.

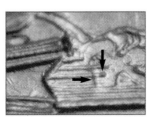

Depressions in arrow shafts.

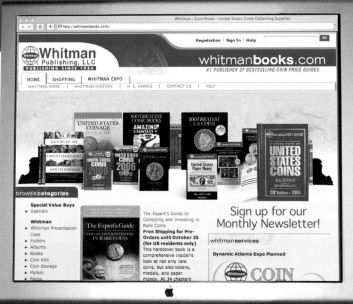
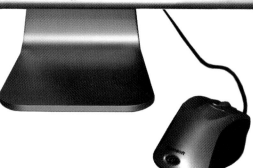

Eagles

Be sure to read the Rules of Thumb on pages 1–9. They contain general guidelines relevant to the study of every counterfeit United States eagle.

You should be aware that many other counterfeit gold coins exist in the market than those covered in this book. The nearly 200 examples described here will educate you on what to look for, but be forewarned that no book will ever be able to illustrate *every* counterfeit.

1799 Capped Bust to Right, Heraldic Eagle $10

Obverse: Weak/Fatty (mushy) features. Die scratches through B in LIBERTY. Spike above lower right serif of T in LIBERTY. Inconsistent strength in all details. *Note:* This date is very heavily counterfeited, and several different dies were used for both the obverse and reverse. Diagnostics may vary for different counterfeits. Pay particular attention to the soft, indistinct letters, numbers, and devices.

Obverse

Die scratches through B in LIBERTY.

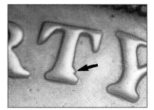

Spike above lower right serif of T in LIBERTY.

Reverse: Weak/Fatty (mushy) features. Depressions above arrow points and above right point of shield. Spikes from upper and lower right serifs of F in OF. "Tiered" (two-level) areas of second T in STATES and first A in AMERICA. Inconsistent strength in all details.

Reverse

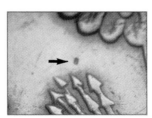

Depression above arrow points.

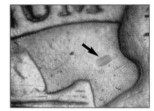

Depression above right point of shield.

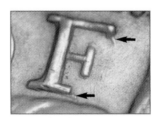

Spikes from F in OF.

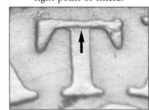

"Tiered" area of second T in STATES.

"Tiered" area of first A in AMERICA.

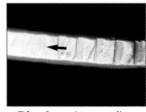

Edge: Inconsistent reeding.

"1872" Liberty Head $10

Reverse: S mintmark removed from field below eagle's tail. *Note:* This is a genuine 1872-S Indian Head eagle, struck in San Francisco, altered outside the Mint to make it look like a Philadelphia strike.

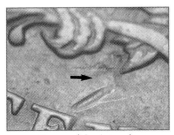

Removed S mintmark.

Reverse

1882 Liberty Head $10

Obverse: Tool marks in hair above ER in LIBERTY. Long tool mark in field between fifth and sixth stars on left.

Obverse

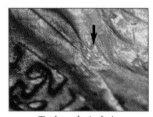

Tool marks in hair.

Tool marks in field.

Reverse: Tool marks (spikes) all around rim at K-6; around CA in AMERICA; and around arrow tips. Weak center design in shield. Arced tool marks around last S in STATES.

Reverse

Tool marks at K-6.

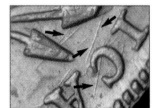

Tool marks around
CA in AMERICA and
around arrow tips.

Weak center design in shield.

Tool marks around
last S in STATES.

1893 Liberty Head $10 (Example 1)

Obverse: Depression below bust, above 9 in date. Tool marks below ear.
Depression in field between bun and third star on right.

Depression below bust.

Obverse

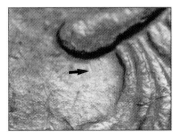

Tool marks below ear.

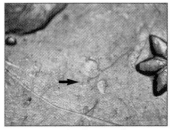

Depression between bun
and third star on right.

Reverse: Weak/Fatty details. Two depressions in field to left of eagle's right leg, and
at top left of first T in STATES. Raised blem between R and U in TRUST,
on banner.

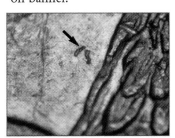

Depressions in field to
left of eagle's right leg.

Reverse

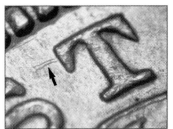

Depressions at top left
of first T in STATES.

Raised blem between
R and U in TRUST.

143

1893 Liberty Head $10 (Example 2)

Obverse: Depressions in field in front of hair, below tiara; in field in front of neck; and to right of lowest hair curl on neck. Blem under chin. Metal fill in bottom of top loop and all of lower loop of 9 in date.

Obverse

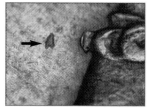

Depression in front of hair.

Depression in front of neck.

Depression on neck.

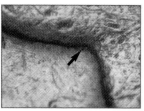

Blem under chin.

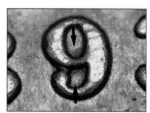

Metal fill in 9 in date.

Reverse: Weak/Fatty details. Depression and tool marks in field between T in TEN and berry. Depressions below eagle's right claw and on center branch, over arrow feather. Depression in field near T in UNITED and to right of butt of branch. *Note:* This is a common false reverse die used on many counterfeit Liberty Head eagles (see also 1899, and 1906 Example 2).

Reverse

Depression and tool marks in field; depressions below eagle's right claw and on center branch.

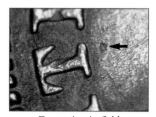

Depression in field near T in UNITED.

Depression to right of butt of branch.

1897-S Liberty Head $10

Obverse: Heavy tool marks throughout design.

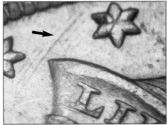

Tool marks above point of tiara.

Obverse

Tool marks near rim.

Reverse: Heavy tool marks throughout design.

Tool marks around denomination.

Reverse

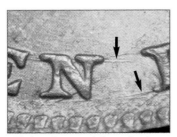

Tool marks around denomination.

1899 Liberty Head $10

Obverse: Weak/Fatty features. Raised blem in field behind bun. Spikes through dentils above second and third stars on left. Depressions above eye. Raised tool marks over date.

Obverse

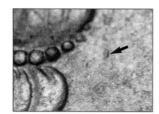

Raised blem behind bun.

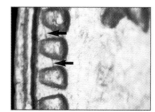

Spikes through dentils above second and third stars on left.

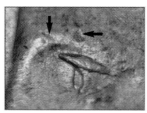

Depressions above eye.

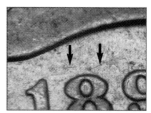

Raised tool marks over date.

Reverse: Weak/Fatty details. Depression and tool marks in field between T in TEN and berry. Depression below eagle's right claw and on center branch, over arrow feather. Depression in field under T in UNITED and to right of butt of branch. *Note:* This is a common false reverse die used on many counterfeit Liberty Head eagles (see also 1893 Example 2, and 1906 Example 2).

Reverse

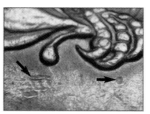

Depression and tool marks in field; depressions below eagle's right claw and on center branch.

Depression in field near T in UNITED.

Depression to right of butt of branch.

1901-S Liberty Head $10

Obverse: Weak/Fatty details. Blem on first star on right. Tool marks and depression on lower bust, and bump where bust meets field. Four depressions behind hanging curl on neck.

Blem on first star on right.

Obverse

Tool marks and depression
on lower bust; bump on bust.

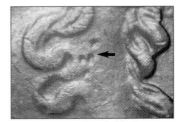

Depressions behind
hanging curl on neck.

Reverse: Weak/Fatty details. Blem lines from eagle's right claw through S mint-mark. Raised tool mark from upper inside of eagle's right wing. Thin tool mark running right from last S in STATES. *Note:* The mark in the field above U in TRUST is a contact mark and not a counterfeit diagnostic.

Blem lines from eagle's right
claw through S mintmark.

Reverse

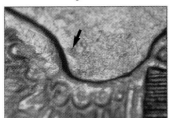

Raised tool mark from upper
inside of eagle's right wing.

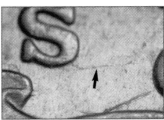

Tool mark running right
from last S in STATES.

147

1906 Liberty Head $10 (Example 1)

Obverse: Depression below 0 in date, near dentils. Blem between 9 and 0 in date. Spikes from dentils around entire obverse. Spikes at top of head where it joins tiara. Blem in field to right of lowest part of bun.

Obverse

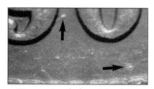

Depression below 0 in date; blem between 9 and 0.

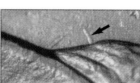

Spike from top of head.

Spikes from dentils; spike from top of head at tiara.

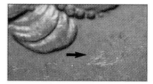

Blem to right of lowest part of bun.

Reverse: Large depressions in field between wing and E in UNITED. Large depression between eagle's beak and wing. Spikes through entire UNITED STATES of AMERICA, especially through AT, last S in STATES, and E in AMERICA. Depression under D in UNITED.

Reverse

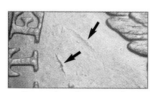

Depressions between wing and E in UNITED.

Spike through AT in STATES.

Spike through E in AMERICA.

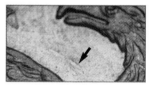

Depression between eagle's beak and wing.

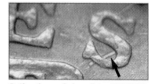

Spike through last S in STATES.

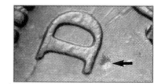

Depression under D in UNITED.

1906 Liberty Head $10 (Example 2)

Obverse: Depression at back of neck between hair curls. Two depressions above eye, below hairline.

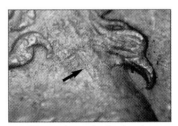

Depression at back of neck.

Obverse

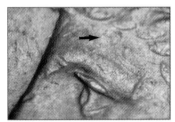

Depressions above eye.

Reverse: Weak/Fatty details. Depression and tool marks in field between T in TEN and berry. Depression below eagle's right claw and on center branch, over arrow feather. Depression in field under T in UNITED and to right of butt of branch. *Note:* This is a common false reverse die used on many counterfeit Liberty Head eagles (see also 1893 Example 2, and 1899).

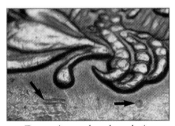

Depression and tool marks in field; depressions below eagle's right claw and on center branch.

Reverse

Depression in field near T in UNITED.

Depression to right of butt of branch.

1907-S Liberty Head $10

Obverse: Weak/Fatty details. Depressions on cheek and jaw; in hair above RT in LIBERTY; and in front of mouth. Depression in field between base of neck and first star on right.

Obverse

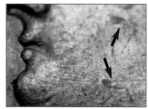

Depressions on cheek and jaw.

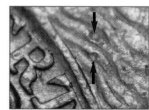

Depressions in hair.

Depression in front of mouth.

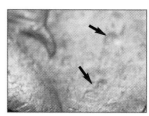

Depression near base of neck.

Reverse: Depression in field between wing and E in UNITED. Raised, irregular line in front of eagle's beak. Depressions between eagle's left leg and arrow points and after last S in STATES.

Reverse

Depression near E in UNITED.

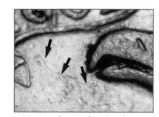

Line in front of eagle's beak.

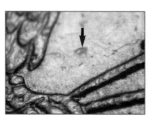

Depression near eagle's leg.

Depression after
last S in STATES.

1908-D Indian Head, No Motto $10

Obverse: Weak/Fatty features. Prooflike surfaces. Tool marks behind neck. Depressions in field northwest of 8 in date, and on nostril.

Tool marks behind neck.

Obverse

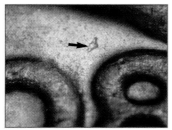

Depression above date.

Depression on nostril.

Reverse: Weak/Fatty features. Prooflike surfaces. Reverse rim much broader than on a genuine coin. Depressions in field below last S in STATES. Large depressions in feathers on eagle's leg, and in field in front of it.

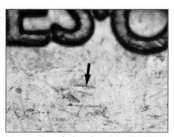

Depressions below last S in STATES.

Reverse

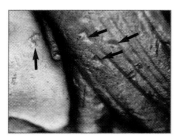

Depressions on and near eagle's leg.

1908 Indian Head, With Motto $10 (Example 1)

Obverse: Depression in center of 1 in date.

Obverse

Depression on 1 in date.

Reverse: Rim depressions over ED and S in UNITED STATES. Depressions in field above N in IN (opposite eagle's right wing), and near M in UNUM. *Note:* This is a common false reverse die used on other counterfeit Indian Head eagles (see also 1932 Example 2).

Reverse

Depressions on rim.

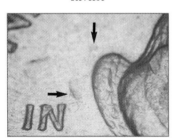

Depressions near wing.

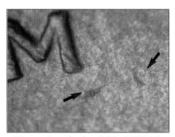

Depressions by last M in UNUM.

1908 Indian Head, With Motto $10 (Example 2)

Obverse: Weak/Fatty details. Prooflike surfaces, but rough, textured fields. Tool marks beneath date.

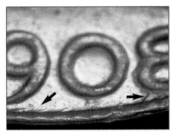

Tool marks beneath date.

Obverse

Reverse: Weak/Fatty details. Raised blems above W in WE. Tool marks throughout lower leaves, under arrow shafts, and through E PLURIBUS UNUM.

Blems above W in WE.

Reverse

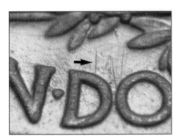

Tool marks throughout lower leaves and under arrows.

Edge: Reeded. *Note:* A genuine coin would have a starred edge.

Tool marks through E PLURIBUS UNUM.

1908-D Indian Head, With Motto $10

Obverse: Weak/Fatty details. Prooflike surfaces. Tool lines behind neck. Depression in upper loop of 8 in date. Depression on upper lip.

Obverse

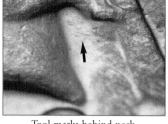

Tool marks behind neck.

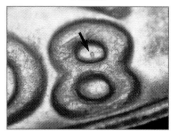

Depression in 8 in date.

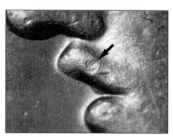

Depression on upper lip.

Reverse: Weak/Fatty details. Prooflike surfaces. Depression under first A in AMERICA. Depression at rim under eagle's wing, at K-4. Many fine, raised lines throughout entire left field.

Reverse

Depression under first A in AMERICA.

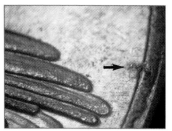

Depression at K-4.

Lines throughout left field.

1910 Indian Head $10

Obverse: Many spikes from rim, from K-11 to K-1, especially at K-12.

Spikes from K-11 to K-1.

Obverse

Reverse: Depression under last A in AMERICA. Depression below second U in UNUM, on eagle's upper wing.

Depression under
last A in AMERICA.

Reverse

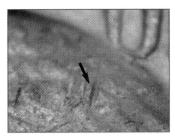

Depression on eagle's upper wing.

1915 Indian Head $10

Obverse: Weak/Fatty features. Depression under eye.

Obverse

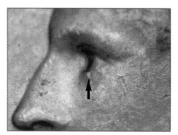

Depression under eye.

Reverse: Spikes by tail at K-4. Weak or missing upper tail feathers near eagle's body.

Reverse

Spikes at K-4.

Edge: Inconsistent spacing of stars.

Weak or missing upper tail feathers.

1915-S Indian Head $10

Obverse: Long, depressed groove below first star on right. Depressions between fourth and fifth stars on right, and above first star on left. Depression on cheek. Doubled 5 in date.

Groove below first star on right.

Depression between fourth and fifth stars on right.

Obverse

Depression above first star on left.

Depression on cheek.

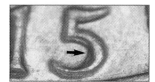

Doubled 5 in date.

Reverse: Tool marks over T in UNITED and through TEN·D in denomination. Depression near T of TEN. Tool marks over AMERICA, near rim. Raised blem in field between eagle's legs. Depression in field to lower right of last T in TRUST.

Tool marks over T in UNITED.

Tool marks though TEN·D; depression under T.

Reverse

Tool marks over AMERICA.

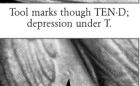

Blem between eagle's legs.

Depression near last T in TRUST.

Edge: "Wandering" stars (some also doubled).

157

1916-S Indian Head $10

Obverse: Three small depressions in field below chin. Tool marks on jaw.

Obverse

Depressions in field below chin.

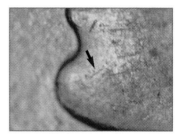

Tool marks on jaw.

Reverse: Pair of depressions by leaves. Depressions behind eagle's head. *Note:* This is a common false reverse used on many counterfeit S-mint Indian Head eagles. Later die states of this counterfeit die show tool marks through the depressions.

Reverse

Tool marks by leaves.

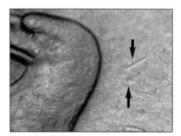

Depressions behind eagle's head.

1932 Indian Head $10 (Example 1)

Obverse: Extreme sharpness in all details. Prooflike fields. *Note:* Made from a hand-cut die.

Obverse

Reverse: Extreme sharpness in all details. Prooflike fields. *Note:* Made from a hand-cut die.

Detail of reverse.

Reverse

1932 Indian Head $10 (Example 2)

Obverse: Raised tool mark under 2 in date.

Obverse

Tool mark under 2 in date.

Reverse: Depression in field by wing. Two depressions by M in UNUM.
Note: This is a common false reverse die used on other counterfeit
Indian Head eagles (see also 1908, With Motto, Example 1).

Reverse

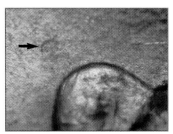

Depression near wing.

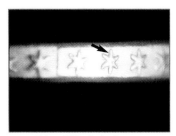

Edge: "Wandering" stars.
Note: This is a common edge
used on several dates of
counterfeit Indian Head eagles.

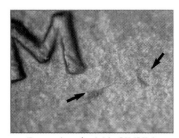

Depressions by M in UNUM.

A GUIDE BOOK OF
—— DOUBLE EAGLE GOLD COINS ——

In the field of United States gold, double eagles are without question the cream of the crop. With their grand size and hefty weight, these large coins are the most popular of America's gold pieces. However, there is more to like about double eagles than just their impressive physical substance. Quite simply, they are beautiful coins. The Saint-Gaudens series in particular, minted from 1907 to 1933, is widely regarded to feature the most attractive United States coinage design. Double eagles also bear testament to a rich and colorful history, from their popularity in the Old West to the relatively new status of certain Liberty Head double eagles as romanticized "treasure ship" coins.

A Guide Book of Double Eagle Gold Coins, written by Q. David Bowers—one of the legends of numismatics—is your complete history and price guide for these amazing pieces of America's past.

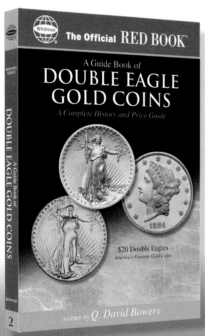

- 296 pages, including an eight-page color spread

- Year-by-year historical analysis of every double eagle, including varieties

- Comprehensive pricing for multiple grades

- Complete mintage figures

- Certified population reports

Double Eagles

Be sure to read the Rules of Thumb on pages 1–9. They contain general guidelines relevant to the study of every counterfeit United States double eagle.

You should be aware that many other counterfeit gold coins exist in the market than those covered in this book. The nearly 200 examples described here will educate you on what to look for, but be forewarned that no book will ever be able to illustrate *every* counterfeit.

Note: While today most counterfeit gold pieces are manufactured to deceive coin collectors – capitalizing on their numismatic value – some double eagles may have been produced with gold fineness of less than .900, to defraud bullion investors.

1856 Liberty Head $20

Obverse: Wrong color. Granular surface. Soft, raised blem on throat, and raised arcs to right. Depression on cheek. Depression under bust, above 8 in date. Depression over I in LIBERTY. Depressions in field over coronet, near star.

Obverse

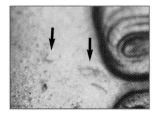

Blem and arcs on throat.

Depression on cheek.

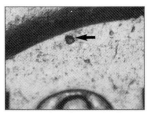

Depression above 8 in date.

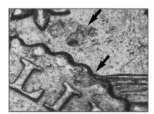

Depression over I in LIBERTY; depressions over coronet.

Reverse: Granular surface. Die break between scrolls, to lower left of shield. Very mushy and weak stars over eagle, especially those within rays.

Reverse

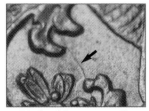

Die break between scrolls.

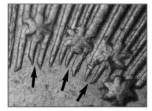

Mushy stars.

Edge: No "draw lines" between reeds (see Appendix B).

1879 Liberty Head $20

Obverse: Raised tool marks in and under E and under T in LIBERTY.

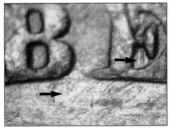

Tool marks in and
under E in LIBERTY.

Obverse

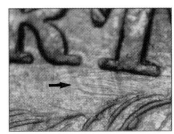

Tool marks under T in LIBERTY.

Reverse: Tool marks in field above D and O in DOLLARS. Small depression in field to right of shield.

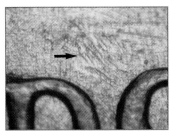

Tool marks above D
and O in DOLLARS.

Reverse

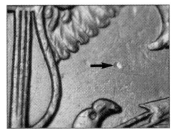

Depression to right of shield.

1894 Liberty Head $20

Obverse: Wrong-style numerals in date. Doubled second star on left. Raised row of dots in right field between hair and first star on right. *Note:* Made from a hand-cut die.

Obverse

Wrong-style numerals in date.

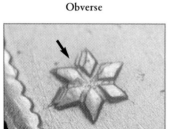

Doubled second star on left.

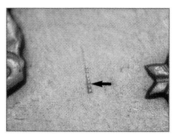

Raised row of dots between hair and first star on right.

Reverse: Tool marks through DOLLARS and in lower right scroll. *Note:* Made from a hand-cut die.

Reverse

Tool marks through DOLLARS and in lower right scroll.

1895 Liberty Head $20

Obverse: Tool marks below date and under bust. Blems (raised lumps) around date.

Tool marks below date and under bust; blems around date.

Obverse

Reverse: Severe, heavy tool marks all over reverse.

Heavy tool marks.

Reverse

1897-S Liberty Head $20

Obverse: Weak/Fatty (mushy) stars and devices. Depressions on eye, cheek, and jaw.

Obverse

Depressions on eye, cheek, and jaw.

Mushy stars.

Reverse: Hand-cut S mintmark was added to the transer die.

Reverse

Hand-cut S mintmark.

1898-S Liberty Head $20

Obverse: Weak/Fatty features. Depressions on nose, cheek, and jaw, and in field above 98 in date. Blem on lower right side of 9 in date.

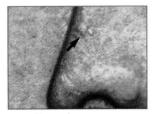

Depression on nose.

Depressions on cheek and jaw.

Obverse

Depression above date.

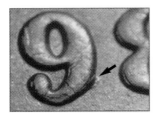

Blem on 9 in date.

Reverse: Weak/Fatty details. Thin, depressed line all around circumference, between dentils and letters. Depression in front of eagle's beak. Thin, raised line from above T to lower part of E in TWENTY. Several small depressions throughout reverse.

Line around circumference.

Depression in front of eagle's beak.

Reverse

Line through letters in TWENTY.

Several depressions throughout.

169

1901-S Liberty Head $20

Obverse: Weak/Fatty details. Fine, raised tool lines all over obverse. Depressions on and below eye; on and in front of face and neck. Blems on first star on left.

Obverse

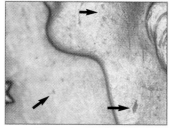

Depressions on and below eye.

Depressions in front of and on face and neck.

Blems on first star on left; tool line to right.

Reverse: Wrong-style ("Blob S") mintmark. Depression above mintmark and rough surface in field. Depressions to right of eagle's head and to left of first S in STATES.

Reverse

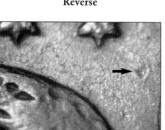

Depression to right of eagle's head.

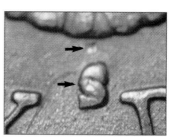

Wrong-style mintmark, with depression above; rough-surfaced field.

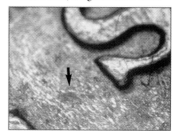

Depression to left of first S in STATES.

1903-S Liberty Head $20

Obverse: Weak/Fatty features. Huge blems in hair, to right of and above LIBERTY. Depressions in front of throat; to upper right of E in LIBERTY; and on eye.

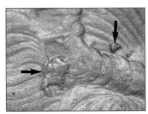

Blems in hair.

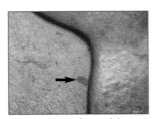

Depression in front of throat.

Obverse

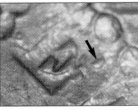

Depression at E in LIBERTY.

Depression on eye.

Reverse: Fine, raised lines around NI in UNITED. Small depressions above R in DOLLARS. Blem to upper right of E in WE.

Lines around NI in UNITED.

Depressions above
R in DOLLARS.

Reverse

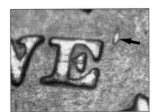

Blem near E in WE.

1904 Liberty Head $20 (Example 1)

Obverse: Weak/Fatty details. Depressions behind neck; in front of nose; and all around second and third stars on left. Large depression by fifth star on right. Depression to left of Y in LIBERTY.

Obverse

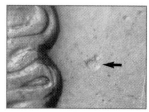

Depression behind neck.

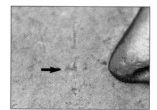

Depression in front of nose.

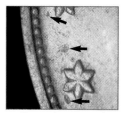

Depressions around third star on left.

Depression by fifth star on right.

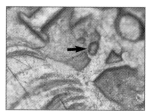

Depression at Y in LIBERTY.

Reverse: Fine tool marks through ED STA and OF in UNITED STATES OF AMERICA. Raised blem to right of eagle's head. Depression under eagle's right wing. Fine, raised line above N in TWENTY.

Reverse

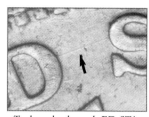

Tool marks through ED STA.

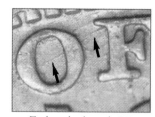

Tool marks through OF.

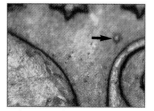

Blem to right of eagle's head.

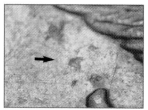

Depression under eagle's wing.

Line above N in TWENTY.

1904 Liberty Head $20 (Example 2)

Obverse: Several short spikes from dentils below date. Depressions on jaw under ear, and on cheek behind flare of nose. Long, thin (raised) tool mark from dentil by third star on left to inner point of second star.

Spikes from dentils below date.

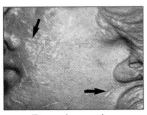

Depressions on jaw and behind nose.

Obverse

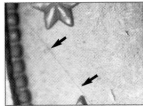

Tool mark from dentil to second star.

Reverse: Two tool lines from ray between T and E in STATES. Several tool marks at M, R, and C in AMERICA. Tool marks over and through UN in UNITED and through almost all reverse dentils.

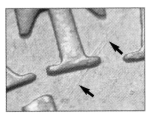

Tool marks around T in STATES.

Tool marks over M in AMERICA.

Reverse

Tool marks over and in R in AMERICA.

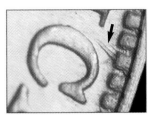

Spike over C in AMERICA.

Tool marks over and through UN in UNITED.

1904 Liberty Head $20 (Example 3)

Obverse: Weak/Fatty details. Tool marks at fourth and fifth stars on left, and under nose. Tool marks in hair above B in LIBERTY.

Obverse

Tool marks at fourth
and fifth stars on left.

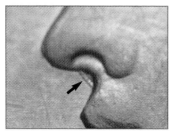

Tool mark under nose.

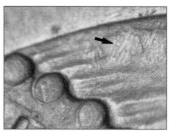

Tool marks in hair.

Reverse: Tool mark at eagle's right wing, near scroll.

Reverse

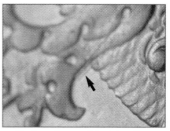

Tool mark at eagle's right wing.

1906 Liberty Head $20

Obverse: Depression to left of Y in LIBERTY.

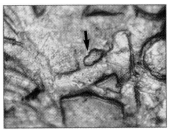

Depression to left of Y in LIBERTY.

Obverse

Reverse: Weak/Fatty details. Long, raised spike from dentils between E and S in STATES to ray. Spike over F in OF. Many small raised blems all over reverse.

Spike at ES in STATES.

Reverse

Spike over F in OF.

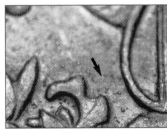

Raised blems.

1907 Liberty Head $20

Obverse: Spikes from dentil at K-10. Raised tool line between first two stars on left. Raised blem by eighth star (over head).

Obverse

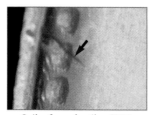

Spike from dentil at K-10.

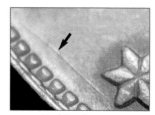

Tool line between first two stars on left.

Blem by star over head.

Reverse: Tool marks above UNITED and between AM in AMERICA. Small depression in field to right of eagle's head. Broken G in GOD.

Reverse

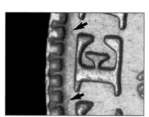

Tool marks above UNITED.

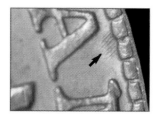

Tool marks above AM in AMERICA.

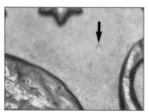

Depression to right of eagle's head.

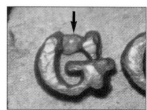

Broken G in GOD.

1907 High Relief Saint-Gaudens $20 (Example 1)

Note: The 1907 High Relief Saint-Gaudens double eagle is a very famous and frequently counterfeited coin. Check carefully any examples you intend to purchase.

Obverse: Tool marks on ray above first M in Roman numeral date, and in hair.

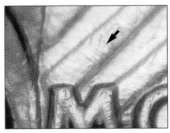

Tool marks on ray
above first M in date.

Obverse

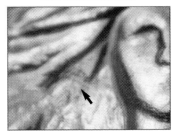

Tool marks in hair.

Reverse: Tool marks between M and E in AMERICA. Design resembling Greek letter omega (Ω) in eagle's claw. *Note:* This omega symbol is a particular counterfeiter's "signature." It is also found on some counterfeit $3 gold pieces.

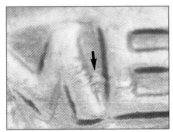

Tool marks between
M and E in AMERICA.

Reverse

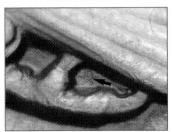

Location of omega symbol.

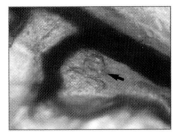

Omega symbol in eagle's claw.

177

1907 High Relief Saint-Gaudens $20 (Example 2)

Note: The 1907 High Relief Saint-Gaudens double eagle is a very famous and frequently counterfeited coin. Check carefully any examples you intend to purchase.

Obverse: Depressions between and over rays under branch, and under VI in date.

Obverse

Depressions between and over rays under branch.

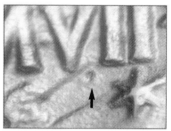

Depression under VI in date.

Reverse: Depression in front of beak. Tool marks between wings and under claw.

Reverse

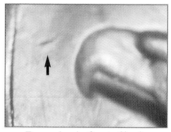

Depression in front of beak.

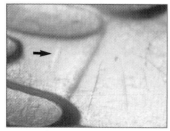

Tool marks between wings.

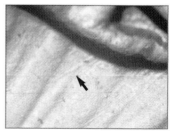

Tool marks under claw.

1910 Saint-Gaudens $20

Obverse: Depressions in field under flowing hair on left; in middle of ray on left; and in center of outstretched arm.

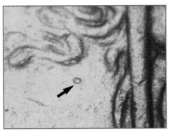

Depression under hair.

Obverse

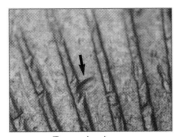

Depression in ray.

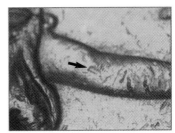

Depression in arm.

Reverse: Depression in field under upper four feathers.

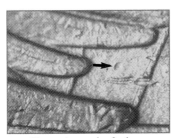

Depression under feathers.

Reverse

1910-D Saint-Gaudens $20

Obverse: Raised lumps inside 0 in date. Doubling of that number to the southeast. Tool mark above second star to left of LIBERTY, near rim. Depression to left of I in LIBERTY. Depression in right field mid-way between branch and stars.

Obverse

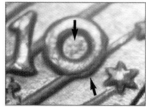

Raised lumps inside 0 in date; doubled 0.

Tool mark above second star to left of LIBERTY.

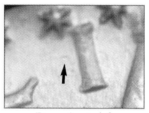

Depression to left of I in LIBERTY.

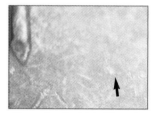

Depression to right of branch.

Reverse: Raised blem between rays under wing.

Reverse

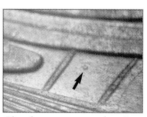

Blem between rays under wing.

1913 Saint-Gaudens $20

Obverse: Details too sharp for this series. Blems on knee and below drapery to left of foot. Depressions on rock under foot.

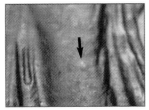

Blem on knee.

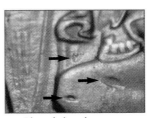

Blems below drapery to left of foot; depressions on rock under foot.

Obverse

Reverse: Large depression on upper (right) wing; blems in center of wing below it, and under back edge, between rays. Depression at tip of longest wing feather. Raised tool marks on rim to left of I in IN, at K-7. Blem on lower portion of fourth ray from left.

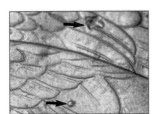

Depression and blem on wings.

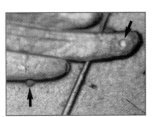

Blem under back wing edge; depression at wing tip.

Reverse

Tool marks on rim to left of I in IN.

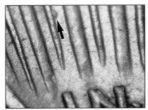

Blem on lower portion of fourth ray from left.

1915-S Saint-Gaudens $20

Obverse: Depressions at lower left of torch; in field midway between T in LIBERTY and shoulder; above third ray to right of Liberty, under arm; and on fourth ray from top, to right of Liberty. Long, thin tool marks throughout upper fields, especially through leaved branch and on Liberty's extended arm.

Reverse

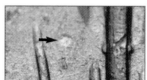

Depression at lower left of torch.

Depression between T in LIBERTY and shoulder.

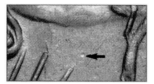

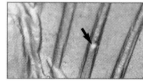

Depression under arm.

Depression on fourth ray from top.

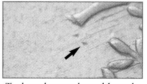

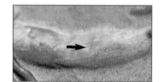

Tool marks near leaved branch.

Tool marks on Liberty's arm.

Reverse: Depressions on sun's ray above WE, and in central area of wing. Depression above eagle's wing, to left of T in TWENTY.

Obverse

Depression on ray above WE.

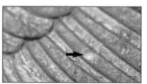

Depression in central area of wing.

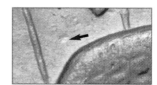

Depression above eagle's wing.

1921 Saint-Gaudens $20

Obverse: Weak/Fatty features. Tool marks around first star on left at bottom; small T to right of this (possibly a counterfeiter's "signature"). Depression under drapery, below rock. Considerably distorted monogram. Depressions to left of L in LIBERTY; spike on I.

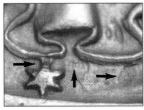

Tool marks and small T at first star on left at bottom; depression under drapery.

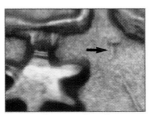

Small T to right of star.

Obverse

Distorted monogram.

Depressions to left of L in LIBERTY; spike on I.

Reverse: Depression on ray above O in GOD; raised blem in gap below and to right of this. Depression in wing, under A in AMERICA.

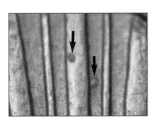

Depression on ray above O in GOD; raised blem in gap to right.

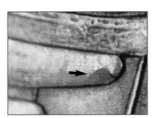

Depression in wing.

Reverse

1922 Saint-Gaudens $20

Obverse: Tool marks at rim to left of rock under drapery, and through leaves under date. Blems on (hidden) right leg. Fine, raised lines all over obverse, especially above Liberty and under arm.

Obverse

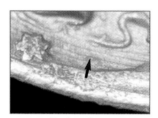

Tool marks at
rim under drapery.

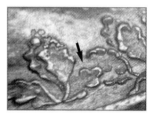

Tool marks through
leaves under date.

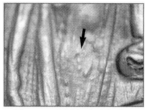

Blems on (hidden) right leg.

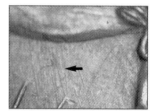

Tool lines under Liberty's
outstretched arm.

Reverse: Fine, raised lines all over reverse. Blem to left of ray at K-3. Weak feather design. All letters "doubled" to the left and/or bottom.

Reverse

Blem to left of ray at K-3.

Doubled letters.

1924 Saint-Gaudens $20 (Example 1)

Obverse: Depression above Liberty's outstretched arm. Small blem on rock below foot. Long tool mark through rays to left of Liberty, near rim at K-8.

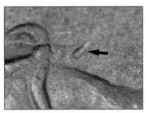

Depression above Liberty's outstretched arm.

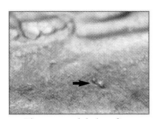

Blem on rock below foot.

Obverse

Tool mark through rays to left of Liberty.

Reverse: Long depression in center of central feather. Depression at tip of same feather. Very shallow depression at lower left side of sun.

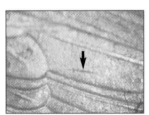

Depression in center of central feather.

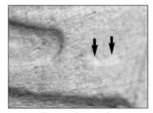

Depression at tip of central feather.

Reverse

Depression at lower left side of sun.

Edge: Many stars and/or letters appear to be falling off edge of coin.

1924 Saint-Gaudens $20 (Example 2)

Obverse: Weak/Fatty (very weak) details; many missing. Fine, raised lines throughout obverse. Very indistinct foot. Poor-quality counterfeit.

Obverse

Indistinct foot.

Weak and missing details.

Reverse: Poor quality. Missing details throughout (note claw, etc).

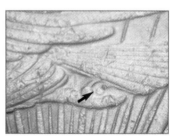

Reverse

Missing details, especially in claw.

1924 Saint-Gaudens $20 (Example 3)

Obverse: Weak/Fatty details. Fine tool lines through branch and lower right obverse, from K-3 to K-5. Three depressions on arm. Depression on center ray to left of Liberty. Depression on base of torch.

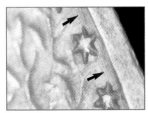

Tool lines through branch.

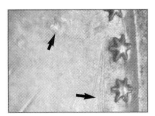

Tool lines from K-3 to K-5.

Obverse

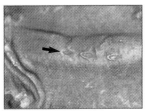

Depressions on arm.

Depressions on center ray to left, and on base of torch.

Reverse: Depression at top of eagle's left wing. Weak letters and small die crack through last A in AMERICA to wing.

Depression at top of wing.

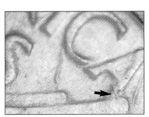

Weak letters; die crack through last A in AMERICA.

Reverse

187

1924 Saint-Gaudens $20 (Example 4)

Obverse: Prooflike surfaces in depressed areas of design. Missing details throughout.

Obverse

Missing details.

Missing details.

Reverse: Depression in front of wing, and in lower ray above GOD.

Reverse

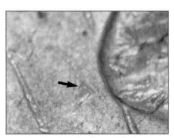

Depression in front of wing.

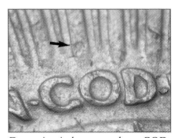

Depression in lower ray above GOD.

1925 Saint-Gaudens $20 (Example 1)

Note: **This is a common obverse/reverse/edge combination used on many counterfeit Saint-Gaudens double eagles.**

Obverse: Weak details. Monogram very mushy. Tool marks under 5 in date.

Weak details.

Obverse

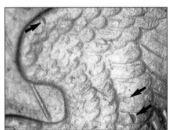

Mushy monogram; weak stars;
tool marks under 5 in date.

Reverse: Depression on top wing and two more in lower part of same wing. Tool lines through O in DOLLARS.

Depressions on top wing.

Reverse

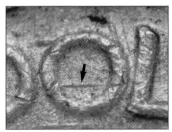

Tool lines through O in DOLLARS.

Edge: Spike on E in
E PLURIBUS UNUM.
(See note on page 191.)

1925 Saint-Gaudens $20 (Example 2)

Obverse: Weak/Fatty (very weak) details. Depression on ray to left of gown. "Blob" monogram. Doubled stars at lower right. Depression on arm.

Obverse

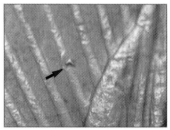

Depression on ray to left of gown.

"Blob" monogram; doubled stars.

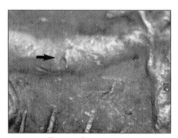

Depression on arm.

Reverse: Depression on long wing feather.

Reverse

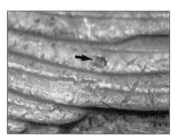

Depression on long wing feather.

1926 Saint-Gaudens $20 (Example 1)

Obverse: Long depression in rays above date.

Depression in rays above date.

Obverse

Reverse: No distinguishing counterfeit diagnostics.

Edge: Spike on E in
E PLURIBUS UNUM. The edge
shown is not the "stock edge" usually
seen an counterfeit Saint-Gaudens
double eagles, which has a thinner,
lighter die scratch from the center
stroke of the E, running northwest.

1926 Saint-Gaudens $20 (Example 2)

Obverse: Weak/Fatty features, especially on head/hair. Depressions below Y in LIBERTY. Small, raised blem near upper right of head.

Obverse

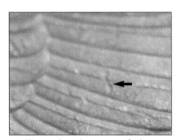

Depression below Y in LIBERTY;
blem near head.

Reverse: Two depressions in center of wing. Depression to far left of sun, under IN. Large depression above third short ray on left.

Reverse

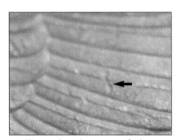

Depressions in center of wing.

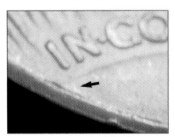

Depression to far left of sun.

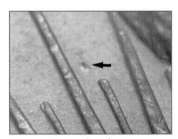

Depression above
third short ray on left.

192

1927 Saint-Gaudens $20

Obverse: Tool marks in field under Liberty's outstretched arm.

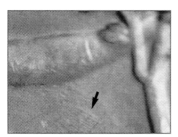

Tool marks under Liberty's
outstretched arm.

Obverse

Reverse: Depression on long wing feather.

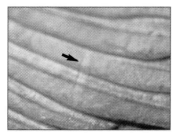

Depression on long wing feather.

Reverse

1927-D Saint-Gaudens $20

Obverse: Raised tool marks under 2 in date. Depression in right field, to right of base of branch.

Obverse

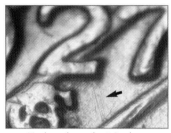
Tool marks under 2 in date.

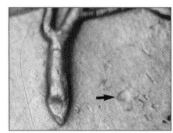
Depression to right of branch.

Reverse: Depressions at lower left edge of sun.

Reverse

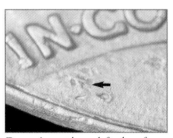
Depressions at lower left edge of sun.

Edge: Fatty, uneven letters.

1929 Saint-Gaudens $20 (Example 1)

Obverse: Prooflike surfaces. Details entirely different from genuine coin.
Note: Made from a hand-cut die.

Detail of obverse.

Obverse

Detail of obverse.

Reverse: Prooflike surfaces. Details entirely different from genuine coin.
Note: Made from a hand-cut die.

Reverse

1929 Saint-Gaudens $20 (Example 2)

Obverse: Tool marks through rays above date and through stars at lower right. Depression on fourth ray on left and blem (raised lump) on next ray to right.

Obverse

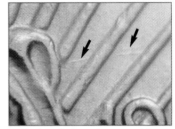

Tool mark through rays at right.

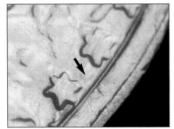

Tool mark through
stars at lower right.

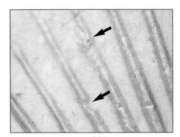

Depression and blem on rays.

Reverse: Long, thin tool mark from O in OF, running southwest through D in DOLLAR.

Reverse

Tool mark running
southwest from O in OF.

Commemoratives

Be sure to read the Rules of Thumb on pages 1–9. They contain general guidelines relevant to the study of every counterfeit United States gold commemorative.

You should be aware that many other counterfeit gold coins exist in the market than those covered in this book. The nearly 200 examples described here will educate you on what to look for, but be forewarned that no book will ever be able to illustrate *every* counterfeit.

1903 Louisiana Purchase Exposition/McKinley $1 (Example 1)

Obverse: Weak/Fatty letters. Details on lapel button not sharp.

Obverse

Weak lapel button details.

Reverse: Weak/Fatty letters and numbers. Tool marks below branch and to right of 3 in date. Filled top of last A in AMERICA, with small blems over it, near dentils. *Note:* This is a common false reverse die used on many counterfeit 1903 Louisiana Purchase/McKinley gold dollars.

Reverse

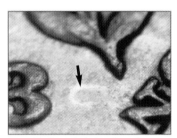

Tool marks below branch.

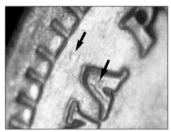

Filled top of last A in AMERICA; small blems near dentils.

1903 Louisiana Purchase Exposition/McKinley $1 (Example 2)

Obverse: Weak/Fatty features. Heart-shaped depression in hair.

Heart-shaped depression in hair.

Obverse

Reverse: Weak/Fatty letters and numbers. Tool marks below branch and to right of 3 in date. Filled top of last A in AMERICA, with small blems over it, near dentils. *Note:* This is a common false reverse die used on many counterfeit 1903 Louisiana Purchase/McKinley gold dollars.

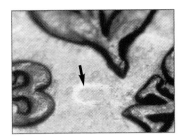

Tool marks below branch.

Reverse

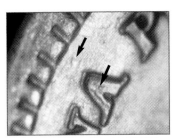

Filled top of last A in AMERICA; small blems near dentils.

1915-S Panama-Pacific Exposition $1

Obverse: Depression on right side of 9 in date. *Note:* The blem (raised die chip) on the cap is on some genuine specimens as well as on some counterfeit coins. The false die was made from a genuine coin with this diagnostic, which was then transferred to the counterfeit pieces.

Obverse

Depression on 9 in date.

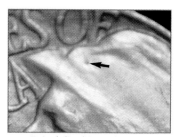

Raised die chip on hat (not necessarily a counterfeit diagnostic).

Reverse: Depressions on D and O in DOLLAR.

Reverse

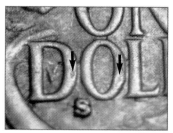

Depressions on D and O in DOLLAR.

1917 McKinley Memorial $1

Obverse: Weak/Fatty details (weak letters). Depression in field between top of head and TA in STATES. Subtle, depressed line from back of bust to O in DOLLAR. Missing right upper portion of U in UNITED. Bifurcated ("fishtail") bottoms of letters. Series of long, fine tool lines between ERICA (in AMERICA) and rim.

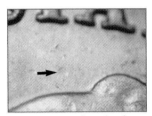

Depression above head.

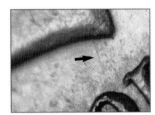

Line from back of bust to O in DOLLAR.

Obverse

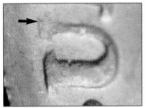

Incomplete U in UNITED.

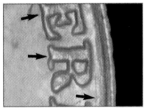

Bifurcated bottoms of letters; tool lines between ERICA (in AMERICA) and rim.

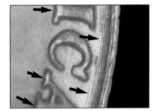

Bifurcated bottoms of letters; tool lines between ERICA (in AMERICA) and rim.

Reverse: Long, fine tool lines over NL in McKINLEY. No die polishing marks below steps (unlike a genuine specimen, which would have these).

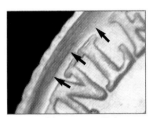

Tool lines over NL in McKinley.

Absent die polishing marks below steps.

Reverse

201

1922 Grant Memorial $1

Obverse: Depressions in field below 22 in 1822; between D and O in DOLLAR; and below A in GRANT. Tool marks around rim at K-9, above NITE in UNITED.

Obverse

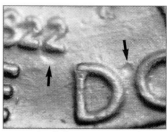

Depression below 22 in 1822; depression between D and O in DOLLAR.

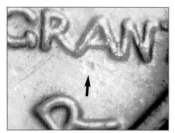

Depression below A in GRANT.

Tool marks around rim at K-9.

Reverse: Spikes around rim at K-9 and between WE and TRUST.

Reverse

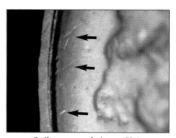

Spikes around rim at K-9.

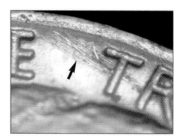

Spikes between WE and TRUST.

1926 Sesquicentennial of Independence $2.50

Obverse: Depressions in ER in AMERICA and in field under point of robe.

Depression in ER in AMERICA.

Obverse

Depression under point of robe.

Reverse: Depression above US in PLURIBUS, at base of Independence Hall.

Depression above US in PLURIBUS.

Reverse

Discover the World of Money

As a Member of the AMERICAN NUMISMATIC ASSOCIATION

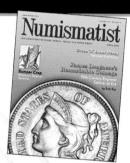

The American Numismatic Association — a non-profit, educational organization — encourages people to study and collect money and related items. From beginner to expert, celebrity to financier, individuals with common interests and unique resources connect at the ANA.

1 YEAR OF MEMBERSHIP MEANS BIG REWARDS.

- **12** issues of *Numismatist* magazine delivered to your door.
- Mediation and consumer advocate **assistance**.
- Members-only **discounts**.

MEMBERSHIP

- ○ One-Year Regular, $36
- ○ Two-Year Regular, $70
- ○ One-Year Senior, $31 *(65 and older)*
- ○ Two-Year Senior, $60 *(65 and older)*

 Yes! Please make me a member of America's premiere numismatic association.

NAME: _____ DATE OF BIRTH: _____
(For senior discount)

ADDRESS: _____ CITY: _____ STATE: ____ ZIP: _____

PHONE: _____ E-MAIL: _____

Please accept my application for membership in the ANA, subject to the bylaws of the Association. I also agree to abide by the Code of Ethics adopted by the Association.
○ Periodically, the ANA's mailing list is sold or provided to third parties. If you do not want your information provided for non-ANA-related mailings, please check here.

PLEASE CHARGE MY: ○ Visa ○ Mastercard ○ AmEx ○ Discover

Card Number: _____ Exp. Date: _____

Cardholder Signature: _____

OR Send Check, payable to:
American Numismatic Association
818 N. Cascade Ave.
Colorado Springs, CO 80903
800-367-9723 • www.money.org

Join online at www.money.org!

WHC

California Gold Pieces

Be sure to read the Rules of Thumb on pages 1–9. They contain general guidelines relevant to the study of every counterfeit California gold piece.

You should be aware that many other counterfeit gold coins exist in the market than those covered in this book. The nearly 200 examples described here will educate you on what to look for, but be forewarned that no book will ever be able to illustrate *every* counterfeit.

Various dates (1852, 1854, 1856, etc.)
Round or octagonal. Most have no gold content.

Obverse: Might have a Liberty Head or Indian Head design; a few are dated 1872 and feature the head of George Washington.

Fantasy California gold piece obverse.　　Fantasy California gold piece obverse.　　Fantasy California gold piece obverse.

Reverse: Usually (but not always) depicts a walking bear, with only ¼ or ½ (and no denomination unit). *Note:* If a piece does not have the denomination on the reverse expressed as CENTS, DOL, DOLL, or DOLLAR, it is not genuine.

Fantasy California gold piece reverse.　　Fantasy California gold piece reverse.　　Fantasy California gold piece reverse.

1854 Kellogg & Co. $20

Obverse: Many small raised "pimples" over entire surface. *Note:* This is a cast counterfeit.

Closeup of date.

Obverse

Closeup of tiara.

Reverse: Many small raised "pimples" over entire surface. *Note:* This is a cast counterfeit.

Closeup of shield area.

Reverse

Weights and Tolerances for United States Gold Coins

TYPE	GRAMS WT.	TOLERANCE	GRAINS WT.	TOLERANCE
Gold Dollar				
1849–1854 (Liberty Head)	1.672	0.016	25.80	0.25
1854–1889 (Indian Princess Head)	1.672	0.016	25.80	0.25
1903–1922 (commemoratives)	1.672	0.016	25.80	0.25
Quarter Eagle ($2.50)				
1796–1807 (Capped Bust to Right)	4.374		67.50	
1808 (Capped Bust to Left)	4.374		67.50	
1821–1827 (Capped Head to Left, Large Diameter)	4.374		67.50	
1829–1834 (Capped Head to Left, Reduced Diameter)	4.374		67.50	
1834–1836 (Classic Head)	4.180	0.008	64.50	0.13
1837–1839 (Classic Head)	4.180	0.016	64.50	0.25
1840–1907 (Liberty Head)	4.180	0.016	64.50	0.25
1908–1929 (Indian Head)	4.180	0.016	64.50	0.25
$3 Gold Piece				
1854–1873 (Indian Princess Head)	5.015		77.40	
1873–1889 (Indian Princess Head)	5.015	0.016	77.40	0.25
$4 Stella (Pattern) (unofficial data)				
1879–1880	7.000		108.026	21.59
Half Eagle ($5)				
1795–1807 (Capped Bust to Right)	8.748		135.00	
1807–1812 (Capped Bust to Left)	8.748		135.00	
1813–1834 (Capped Head to Left)	8.748		135.00	
1834–1836 (Classic Head)	8.359	0.017	129.00	0.26
1837–1838 (Classic Head)	8.359	0.016	129.00	0.25
1839–1849 (Liberty Head)	8.359	0.016	129.00	0.25
1849–1873 (Liberty Head)	8.359	0.032	129.00	0.50
1873–1929 (Liberty Head and Indian Head)	8.359	0.016	129.00	0.25
1986 to date (commemoratives)	8.359	0.042	129.00	0.65
Eagle ($10)				
1795–1804 (Capped Bust to Right)	17.496		270.00	
1838–1849 (Liberty Head)	16.718	0.016	258.00	0.25
1849–1873 (Liberty Head)	16.718	0.032	258.00	0.50
1873–1933 (Liberty Head and Indian Head)	16.718	0.088	258.00	0.50
1984 to date (commemoratives)	16.718	0.088	258.00	1.36
Double Eagle ($20)				
1850–1907 (Liberty Head)	33.436	0.032	516.00	0.50
1907–1933 (Saint-Gaudens)	33.436	0.032	516.00	0.50

Diameters of United States Gold Coins

TYPE	DIAMETER
Gold Dollar	
1849–1854 (Liberty Head)	13 mm
1854–1889 (Indian Princess Head)	15 mm
1903–1922 (commemoratives)	15 mm
Quarter Eagle ($2.50)	
1796–1807 (Capped Bust to Right)	~20 mm
1808 (Capped Bust to Left)	~20 mm
1821–1827 (Capped Head to Left, Large Diameter)	~18.5 mm
1829–1834 (Capped Head to Left, Reduced Diameter)	18.2 mm
1834–1839 (Classic Head)	18.2 mm
1840–1907 (Liberty Head, all varieties)	18 mm
1908–1929 (Indian Head)	18 mm
$3 Gold Piece	
1854–1889 (Indian Princess Head)	20.5 mm
$4 Stella (Pattern)	
1879–1880	22 mm
Half Eagle ($5)	
1795–1807 (Capped Bust to Right)	~25 mm
1807–1812 (Capped Bust to Left)	~25 mm
1813–1834 (Capped Head to Left)	~25 mm
1834–1836 (Classic Head)	23.8 mm
1837–1838 (Classic Head)	22.5 mm
1839–1908 (Liberty Head, all varieties)	21.6 mm
1908–1929 (Indian Head)	21.6 mm
1986 to date (commemoratives)	21.6 mm
Eagle ($10)	
1795–1804 (Capped Bust to Right)	~33 mm
1838–1907 (Liberty Head, all varieties)	27 mm
1907–1933 (Indian Head)	27 mm
1984 to date (commemoratives)	27 mm
Double Eagle ($20)	
1850–1907 (Liberty Head)	34 mm
1907–1933 (Saint-Gaudens)	34 mm

The following are features that are found on genuine United States gold coins. Note that some of these features are not necessarily a guarantee that a coin is authentic. All of the photographs below are of genuine U.S. gold coins.

1. Crisp, sharp letters and devices. Note that all letters, numbers, and devices are well defined and "squared off," unlike those of most counterfeit pieces made from transfer dies, which have weak or fat ("mushy") letters, etc.

Crisp, sharp letters in UNITED,
on a genuine coin

Crisp, sharp letters in AMERICA,
on a genuine coin

2. Contact marks. "Bag marks" on genuine coins usually exhibit shiny depressions and sharp edges, from contact with another coin or a sharp object. On counterfeit coins made from transfer dies, these translate into muted or "soft" depressions with rounded edges, and have the same texture and look as the surrounding area.

Contact marks on a genuine coin

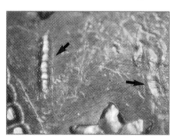

Contact marks on a genuine coin

3. Die polishing marks. When well defined and in recessed areas of a design (such as the area surrounding the word LIBERTY in the tiara), die polishing marks are usually an indication of a genuine coin.

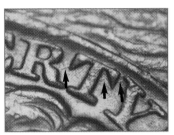

Die polishing marks
on a genuine coin

Die polishing mark
on a genuine coin

Die polishing marks
on a genuine coin

4. Die cracks. These occur on genuine coins through the normal extended use of the die(s). Their presence on a coin is a good sign that it is genuine.

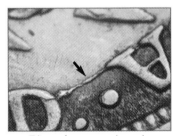

Die crack on a genuine coin

Die cracks on a genuine coin

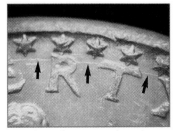

Die cracks on a genuine coin

5. "Draw lines" in the reeding. These are fine, straight lines between the reeds on the edge of a coin, formed when the coin is forced out of the reeded collar by the lower die. Counterfeit coins quite often do not show these characteristics.

"Draw lines" in the reeding
of a genuine coin

6. Clash marks. These occur when the two dies come together without a planchet between them, and impress portions of their design on each other. Sharp, crisp clash marks are usually a good indication that a coin is genuine. Any clash marks on the host coin transferred to the counterfeit die will usually be "mushy" and not sharp. In this photograph, on the Indian's throat you can see the eagle's wing, breast, and neck design from the reverse.

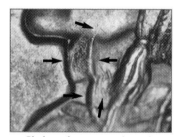

Clash marks on a genuine coin

Southern Gold Society

FOUNDED 2001

The Southern Gold Society was formed to increase the enjoyment and study of Southern gold coins and related history, through an informal, relaxed mix of education and fellowship.

It is reminiscent of the societies of a bygone era, offering an environment wherein connoisseurship and a gentlemanly appreciation of Southern gold coins is the order of the day.

Purpose:

- To facilitate the enjoyment and study of the gold coins and related history of the Southern branch mints (Dahlonega, Charlotte, and New Orleans) and private Southern minters (Templeton Reid and the Bechtlers).

- To enjoy each member's knowledge and friendship in an informal manner.

- To provide a relaxed, pleasant environment in which to meet during selected coin shows and other convenient events.

- To encourage the appreciation and preservation of a Southern gold coin's original surfaces.

- To consolidate the information, resources, and talent available to enthusiasts of these historic Southern gold coins.

Visit us online at www.southerngoldsociety.org.